VISCOUNT CECIL

THE
WAY OF PEACE

Essays and Addresses

BY

VISCOUNT CECIL

LONDON

PHILIP ALLAN & CO. LTD.

QUALITY HOUSE, GREAT RUSSELL STREET, W.C. 1

First Edition in 1928

341.22

PRINTED IN GREAT BRITAIN BY ROBERT MACLEHOSE AND CO. LTD.
THE UNIVERSITY PRESS, GLASGOW.

I AM greatly indebted for permission, kindly given to me, to republish certain of these essays and addresses : to the Editor of the *Quarterly Review*, for the essay on the " Party System " ; to the Editor of *The Spectator* for the essay on " The League in Retrospect " ; to the University College, London, for the Rickman Godlee Lecture on " The Genesis of Co-operation " ; to the Lindsey Press for the address on " The Moral Basis of the League of Nations " ; to the Trustees, and the Delegates of the Oxford University Press, for the Burge Memorial Lecture (1920) on " International Arbitration " ; to the University College Union Society for the address on " The Future of the League " ; and to the World Peace Foundation for that on " Disarmament and the League." The articles and addresses are printed substantially as they first appeared.

CECIL

CONTENTS

I

INTRODUCTORY

(1928)

THE papers contained in this volume were all composed during the last ten years. They do not pretend to set out a political creed. But it is believed that they have a certain unity of thought and that they express a point of view held by a considerable number of persons at the present day.

From one point of view it may be said that the late war made little change in our national life, except upon the economic side. The same problems, social, political, intellectual, moral, religious, are still with us. Certain questions such as Home Rule and the disendowment of the Welsh Church have been disposed of. But they were nearly finished in 1914. Women have got the vote, the Labour Party has held office, the House of Lords has decayed, the Liberal Party is distracted. These changes may have been hastened by the war, but before the war they were all on the way. Nevertheless, for many of us the situation is fundamentally altered. We have seen what modern war is. Till it occurred we had no real conception of what it meant. I remember before the war reading a little book of sketches of what a future war would be like, called *The Green Curve*. It was vividly written, but I am afraid I put it aside as fantastically alarmist. In point of fact it greatly understated the truth. We now know from actual experience the vast mass of misery which war can inflict. We have seen something of it even in our own country, and we are aware that in other countries the suffering has been far greater. No doubt we cannot grasp the full extent of the material disaster that has occurred. The figures of killed and wounded, of towns and villages destroyed, of wealth consumed, are so enormous that no adequate mental image can be formed of them. Even so the impression has been terrific. It has shaken to its foundations all the assumptions and axioms upon which we used to carry on our lives.

There are some who believe that terrible as has been the material injury, there has been great compensation in the strengthening of the moral fibre of the race. I can see no sufficient evidence to support this belief. On the contrary, morality and religion seem to be weaker than they were, luxury and vice more rampant.

One consequence of the convulsion should be specially noted by Conservatives. Revolution is the child of war. It always has been so, and no better example of this truth could be found than that which we have seen in the last few years. In three of the four Central Powers there has been a complete break with the past. Austria-Hungary has ceased to exist and the House of Hapsburg has been driven from the throne. So has the House of Hohenzollern in Germany, which has become a republic. In Turkey the whole of the ancient system including the Khalifate has disappeared. Bulgaria has escaped great constitutional changes, but only by the skin of its teeth. Nor have political upheavals been confined to the defeated countries. Russian Bolshevism existed before 1914, but it was the war which enabled it to seize supreme power. So, too, the series of Greek revolutions culminating in the present republic there, were all the outcome of war. Even a victorious power like Italy only avoided a revolution to the left by accepting a revolution to the right ; and neutral Spain may be said to have followed suit. True, France and England have escaped revolution, but there were ominous signs in both countries during the years 1919-20. Had the fortune of war been different, who can say what might have happened to the political stability of our own island ?

Politically then no less than physically the destructive consequences of modern war are incalculable. No other material evil is comparable to it. That is the lesson which the four years of horror and their sequel have burnt into our consciousness. It has not necessarily changed our opinions, but it has altered their values. For the sake of illustration may I take my own case ? I still hold that Home Rule was not the best solution of the Irish question, and that the religious grievances of Wales could have been met without transferring endowments from sacred to secular purposes. I am still unconvinced of the wisdom of the budget of 1910 or of the Parliament Act. Nor can I see that a case has been made out for far-reaching fiscal change. But all these things seem to me now of relatively minor importance. I am quite ready to believe that the Government schemes for derating and reform of local government are right and proper. I doubt the wisdom of any great extension of public ownership of industry. But important though these things may be, neither the future of the world nor even of this country can be thought to depend upon their adoption or rejection. They may or may not be improvements, but they are only of secondary value so long as the peace of the world is still in doubt. How can peace be preserved ? Is there any other way except through the League of Nations, and if not what can we do to support and strengthen the League ? These are the burning political questions of the day compared with which all others pale into insignificance.

Not that I am a fanatical admirer of the League of Nations or think it incapable of improvement. If I may be allowed to say so, I know too much about it to hold any such opinion. It is doubtless as full of imperfections as other human institutions. But there it is. It is an organised attempt to secure peace and promote international co-operation ; and no fair-minded man can deny that it has achieved a

considerable measure of success. In spite of all its
failures, real and alleged, it has steadily grown in
public estimation. It has at the least made war
more difficult, and international progress easier.

In these circumstances hostile critics, especially
if they are Conservatives, may well be asked—What
is their alternative ? I put aside that infinitesimal
minority which regards war with complacency or
even approval. If the last ten years have not altered
their opinion neither will they be persuaded though
one rose from the dead. But there are others—
men who hate war as much as anyone but yet reject
the League. What is their policy ? Do they propose to do nothing—to take away the League and
put nothing in its place ? That surely is a counsel
of despair. If we are to return simply to pre-war
conditions is it not certain that the causes which have
led to war in the past will lead to war in the future ?
Are we still to pin our faith to preparedness and
alliances after all our centuries of experience of those
broken reeds ? That would indeed be Bourbonism
of the deepest dye. It is sometimes suggested
that our proper course is to withdraw from all continental entanglements and leave Europe to stew in
her own juice. I will say nothing about the morality
of this proposal, though it may perhaps be doubted
whether an egotism which would be shocking in an
individual can be admirable in a nation. Certainly
it is not so that in the past we have understood our
national responsibilities. But whether admirable or

the reverse, the final objection to such a policy is that it is impossible. Never in our history have we been able to stand aloof from European complications. Why did we go to war in 1914 ? Assuredly not because we had a Government of fire-eaters. The Prime Minister, the Chancellor of the Exchequer, the Foreign Secretary differed on many questions. But they all equally hated war. We went to war partly to maintain the public law of Europe, violated by the invasion of Belgium ; but even more because the triumph of the principles against which we fought would have threatened our national and still more our imperial existence. It is no mere rhetorical tag to say that the British Empire is built on liberty and justice. It is an actual fact. Substitute for those agencies force, and the Empire would unquestionably fall to pieces as it very nearly did in the eighteenth century. Bismarck may have been right in founding the German Empire on " blood and iron," though he seems to have had some doubts on the point in his later years. It may have been natural for his successors to think that the same system could be applied to international relations. But it would undoubtedly be fatal to the existence of the British Commonwealth, and this was fully recognised by many of those who directed the policy of our antagonists. To them the British Empire was the symbol of all that they thought most deplorable in international life. Its destruction was one of their chief objects.

In the late war, then, we were fighting in self-defence quite as much as were the French and others of our allies. Yet the immediate cause of the war—a political crime in the south-east corner of Europe—seemed as far removed from our " interests " as anything could be. So in itself it was, but the quarrel about it involved the Continent, and once that happened it was impossible for us to remain at peace. Precisely the same thing happened in the French Revolutionary wars. There has never been a more pacifically inclined British Minister than Pitt, and he did his best to keep out of war. But he failed : events were too strong for him, and for twenty years we were in the forefront of the struggle. It has always been so and it always will be so. If we could not keep out of European entanglements when we were economically self-contained or nearly so, and when the Channel passage was an undertaking not without difficulty and danger, what hope is there for such a policy when our economic and cultural bonds with the Continent have grown so close, and the Channel has become a brief interlude in a journey by land, and not even that if we travel by air ?

No, whether we like it or not, we are part of Europe. We have got to live with her and we had better make the best of it. We should aim not at separation but at closer union. Only so can war be avoided and civilisation saved. The interdependence of nations is the keynote of international life at the present day. That is why we must cultivate an international sense. We must learn to think not only imperially but internationally as well. International organisation is a necessity of modern times, and the League is the only organisation of the kind in being. Granted that it is far from perfect, it would be madness to discard it. Its creation was a step in the right direction. Our business is to carry on the advance. When the Covenant was first laid before the plenary Conference, at Paris, I ventured to say on behalf of the British Government :

" We are not seeking to produce for the world a building finished and complete in all respects. To have attempted such a thing would have been an arrogant piece of folly. All we have tried to do, all we have hoped to do, is to lay soundly and truly the foundations upon which our successors may build."

That seems to me still the right way to look at the Covenant. We have to go on building up international safeguards against war. We cannot afford to rest and be thankful. There is very much to be done. We have got the barest outline of an international organisation, a sketch of an international Parliament, an international executive, an international judiciary and an international civil service, but not more. We have scarcely even laid the foundations of an international police force. We are still slaves to the conception that each nation must arm itself against all the others. That seemed to me the real tragedy of the Naval Conference last year. We went there to carry further the brilliant work done by Lord Balfour and Mr. Hughes at Washington. We loudly proclaimed that war between the United States and ourselves was unthinkable, and yet the whole of the discussion was carried on by both sides upon the basis that such a war might take place. British and American naval experts exhausted their ingenuity in controversies as to whether an excess of power in this kind of ship or that kind of gun might not give to one or the other an advantage if hostilities took place. Nor was that chiefly the fault of the experts. They did what their Governments authorised them to do. They were instructed to advise what would be " safe " for their countries to accept. If they had been told that the two Governments desired to fix a standard of naval preparations and for motives of convenience thought that a rough equality between them should be aimed at—without bothering about minor matters—an agreement would have been easy. It broke down because neither Government was ready to accept arrangements which their experts told them might in certain circumstances give to the other country some possible advantage if in the distant future the almost impossible event of an Anglo-American war took place. International disarmament negotiations carried on in such a spirit as that, with America or others, could never succeed. And yet, as I thought and think, an international

agreement to limit armaments is essential if an
enduring world peace is to be attained. Without
it, competition in armaments is certain to recom-
mence—is indeed recommencing—and with it the
old " preparedness " heresy will again be fastened
on the nations of the world. I recognise that force
may still be an unavoidable element in international
as it is in national life. But it must be the force of
the whole community directed against the law-breaker,
and not legalised international brigandage. National
armaments must be regarded as the contribution of
each state to the force required to preserve the peace
of the world, rather than a precaution necessary for
the national safety. They must be looked on as a
burden and not a privilege, and if their limitation be
approached in that spirit the problem should not be
insoluble.

The attainment of this attitude of mind should be
greatly assisted by the Kellogg Pact. It is true that
it only lays down a principle, and that in the widest
terms. It forbids the use of war as an instrument of
national policy, with an understanding that such a
prohibition does not apply to wars of self-defence.
But it makes no attempt to define the limits of self-
defence : that is left to the wisdom and conscience
of each country. Few countries, however, would
admit that in recent times they have ever fought for
any other motive. That was certainly our chief
reason for going to war in 1914, and all the other
belligerent countries would probably make the same

claim. So that the exception of self-defence cuts very deep into the general prohibition of war. Yet it is an exception that must obviously be made. Self-defence is as much the first law of nature for nations as it is for individuals. Nor is it possible to define self-defence any more than it is possible to define aggression. The Kellogg Pact is therefore unavoidably incomplete. But it is not on that account valueless. To have it explicitly laid down that violence is as inadmissible a resource for nations as for individuals is a great advance in itself, and paves the way for future progress. The next thing is to leave it to some international authority, preferably a judicial tribunal, to say when the right of self-defence has arisen. The acceptance of the jurisdiction of the Permanent Court of International Justice on this point by the signature of the Optional Clause seems an obvious way of reaching the desired end. Further, it would be useful formally to distinguish between public war undertaken in fulfilment of international obligations to safeguard peace and coerce peace-breakers, and private wars waged to impose the will of one nation upon another. It may be said that the words of the Pact restricting the prohibition of war to its use as an instrument of national policy does not forbid and is not intended to forbid wars for public or international purposes. But in a point of such importance it would have been well to use perfectly clear language.

If the Peace Pact is to be effective it must be

accompanied not only by international limitation of armaments but also by the perfecting of other ways of settling international differences. You cannot take away the arbitrament of war and put nothing in its place. It must be said at once that on this point the American scheme is quite inadequate. The general terms of the second clause of the Pact admittedly are of little value. They set up no machinery for the decision of international questions, and without machinery nothing can be done. Nor do the treaties of arbitration and conciliation now being negotiated by the United States carry us much further. They are full of loopholes and practically leave all serious international disputes unprovided for. Moreover, they are only bilateral and do not affect controversies between those nations who are most likely to resort to war. Whether American opinion will allow their Government to go further than this is extremely doubtful. But we in Europe shall be criminal if for ourselves we are satisfied with so insufficient a scheme.

Beyond further progress in the direction of disarmament and pacific settlement of international disputes, there is one other very desirable international reform, and that is the provision of better means for the review of obsolete or unjust treaties. The subject is exceedingly thorny, and in the present state of European opinion must be approached with the greatest caution. It is much too soon to attempt to make any changes in the Paris treaties, even if it were far clearer than it is what those changes ought to be. But there are other cases where treaty revision is called for as, for instance, in China. Article 19 of the Covenant recognises in express terms that the Assembly as the legislative body of the League should recommend the review of treaties in proper cases. But the Article has never been put in operation and no machinery for its use exists. If a motion for the revision of a treaty were made in the Assembly it would under the rules of procedure be sent first to a Committee for examination. None of the ordinary Committees of the Assembly would be suitable for such a function. Some body of a more judicial character would be required. It is to be hoped that this matter will receive careful attention, since it is quite certain that some well thought out means for reconsidering treaties which have become unenforceable is essential if respect for international engagements is to be preserved.

One word in conclusion. The League of Nations is not an end in itself. It exists to make effective the will to peace of the peoples of the world. Unless there is that will to peace the League has no reason for its existence. That is why it is rightly said to be based on Public Opinion. The Covenant with its reiterated insistence on publicity bears witness to the same truth. Without Public Opinion the League can do nothing. If the peoples want war, no League will permanently prevent them from resorting to it. That is why the education of Public Opinion is of such vast importance and why there is such an urgent call to promote the activities of the League of Nations Union and kindred societies here and abroad. Further, it is well to remember that Public Opinion is one. The Will to Peace is one. It is foolish for a man to preach international peace and to advocate industrial war. The arguments against war are no less powerful in the case of classes than of nations. The substituting of force for reason is just as objectionable in one case as in the other, and an acceptance of it as the arbiter of industrial disputes will add to the difficulties of its elimination in the international sphere. That is why I have included in this volume pleas for industrial co-operation—call it co-partnership or what you will. It seemed to me strictly germane to the main subject of the book.

II

THE PARTY SYSTEM AND PEACE

(1925)

THE Party system is one of the recognised " Aunt
Sallys " of our public life. It is, like the police and
the legal profession and female fashions, the object
of much display of contumely and ridicule which has
not, and perhaps is not intended to have, any practical
effect. On the face of it the Party system lends itself
to such treatment. Parties consist of persons who
have agreed to co-operate with one another for political purposes. Some of them have been moved to
do so by profound conviction ; others by class considerations ; others again by hereditary tradition or
economic or even religious comradeship ; others by
the hopes of personal advancement. Yet all necessarily adopt the same language consisting of exaggerated praise of their own Party and unqualified con-
demnation of all others ; even when, as sometimes
happens, the speaker is really indifferent or perhaps
even in his heart inclines to the view which he is
denouncing. This seemingly questionable proceeding is not as bad as it sounds. For as far as the
Opposition Party is concerned, it is or should be, if

15

they are sincere in their political creed, one of their chief objects to turn out the Government. To do so they must devote all their energy to the conversion of Parliament and the electorate to their views. No chance must be missed of belittling the achievements or ridiculing the proposals of the Party in power. If a harassed Minister uses an ambiguous phrase, the meaning likely to be most unpopular must be seized upon and proclaimed throughout the land. Nothing the Cabinet do can be right. If they treat dangers lightly they are frivolous ; if they treat them seriously they are panic-struck ; if they resist a demand they are heartless or perverse ; if they concede it they are weak and cowardly ; and if they seek safety in adopting the policy of their predecessors they are vacillating and unprincipled. Nor can the Ministerialists afford to be backward in the contest. It is their business to keep the Opposition out and themselves in. They must not allow modesty to prevent them from blowing their own trumpets, even if it is likely to be a solo performance. Since the Opposition are debarred from legislative or executive action, criticism of them is not so easy. Still they can be reproached with factiousness and irresponsibility, their internal difficulties can be magnified, their past can be held up to contempt and their future proceedings to horror.

No doubt political controversy is not always conducted on quite so shrill a note as this. It is often more measured and therefore more effective. But whatever its actual form the fundamental anomaly remains that half the best political brains of the day are largely employed not so much in seeking a solution of pressing problems as in criticising the proceedings of the other half.   No doubt this apparently very wasteful proceeding has its advantages.   Party criticism is something more than mere expert exercise of *l'art de dénigrer*.   With all its excesses it does make, or ought to make, improbable gross errors by the Government or reckless commitments by the Opposition.   On the other hand it must be remembered that the administration of a country like ours is a very complicated business requiring for its successful transaction the whole strength and power of the best men that can be found.   Energy expended in the Party battle is taken from that which ought to be employed in the good government of the country.   The efficiency of a departmental Minister is not increased nor is his health improved by attending acrimonious debates in the House, prolonged to the small hours, in addition to the work of his department.   Nature has already given more than one warning, both in this country and abroad, that the strain of carrying on Government in a democracy may easily become too great for human endurance.

It is not the least of the charges that can be properly brought against the Party system that it tends to increase this menace to the future of popular government.   Yet it is perfectly obvious that no system of government, other than complete despotism, can exist at all without parties.   They are to be found, more or less, in every assembly, whether large or small, that has to take corporate action.   There will always be in such bodies one section of opinion that is habitually anxious for action and another which regards caution as the highest wisdom, and a tendency to form groups accordingly will emerge.   Probably, in addition, there will be special classes of questions depending for their decision on common principles other than those of caution or courage, which one division of the body will tend to decide in one way, contrary to the views of another division.   Nor is there any objection to this state of things—it is not only natural, but in itself healthy.   For it is no doubt true " that no men can act with effect who do not act in concert ; that no men can act in concert who do not act with confidence ; that no men can act with confidence who are not bound together by common opinions, common interests, and common affections." Parties, therefore, always have existed and always must exist.   They are an essential condition of co-operation.   But you can have parties without a Party system, that is to say, you can have temporary and unorganised common action between members of a deliberative assembly or of an electoral body without such action being systematised.   That is the actual state of things in a very large number of cases. Wherever, indeed, the business of a body of men is only to come to decisions on questions of action or policy there is no need for any Party system, nor does it ordinarily exist.   For instance, in such a body as the Assembly of the League of Nations, parties in a sense invariably exist.   There are those who wish for a forward policy of the League—those who are fearful that a forward policy may defeat its own ends. In every Assembly I have attended, delegations are found who are ordinarily in favour of action, just as there are other delegations who are afraid of doing too much.   But there is no Party system because the decisions once made are done with altogether.   They have no ulterior consequence on the settlement of the policy of the League.   Each question as it arises can be, and usually is, decided on its own merits. The policy adopted is not the policy of this or that party, but of the League as a whole.

Party and the Party system, therefore, are different things.   Parties are inevitable—the result of the basic fact that human beings tend to think alike and to differ.   But the Party system is another matter.   By the Party system is meant the organisation and consolidation of parties into permanent bodies, bound together by a regular machinery and a corporate existence.   In a parliamentary constitution this arrangement largely results from the necessity of having officers or agents of the Parliament or its electorate to carry on its business.   For in the first place such agents have to be appointed, and in the second if the policy of the country is to be continuous and effective they must be supported.   The machinery for their appointment varies.   Sometimes they are appointed by what is in substance a direct vote, as in the Presidential Election in the United States. There the question put to the electors is—Do you wish Mr. A. or Mr. B. to be President ?   In other cases the choice of the executive is indirect.   Under our constitution we elect a House of Commons, and a Ministry then has to be formed which will be supported by a majority of its Members.   But even so the broad question put to the electors is—Do you desire a Conservative, or a Liberal, or a Labour Government ?   The President or the Government, as the case may be, is the expression or symbol of the desires of the voters on the mass of the political questions of the day complicated by their personal predilections.   It is to obtain this expression whether under the American or the British form of Government that an electoral organisation is almost essential.   In no other way can votes and voters be marshalled and secured.   Electors are only moderately interested in political questions in normal circumstances and have to be persuaded to exercise the franchise.   Hence all the paraphernalia of an election—the meetings, the canvassing, the literature (Heaven save the mark), the " slogans," the processions, the shouting and all the other devices necessary to induce the civilised and educated citizen of the twentieth century to decide which set of persons and principles are most likely to secure the good government of his country.   All these things cost money and effort—in other words require co-ordi-

nated exertion.   Hence the creation of Party organisations, Party newspapers, Party funds, both local
and central.   Nor can these arrangements be confined to the material side of human nature.   There
must be a Party creed and a Party policy to which all
members of the Party must subscribe.   So we hear
of " platforms " and " programmes " ; of the charter
of one Party ; the pure milk of the doctrine of another ;
and the historic principles of a third.   Indeed it
sometimes taxes the ingenuity of the Party orators to
explain what is the exact connection between the
policy they advocate and the principles they profess,
and in what respect these latter differ from those of
one or other of the competing organisations.   The
main thing is to have a Party policy.   It has been
said that it does not so much matter what the members
of a Party say as long as they all say the same thing.
The Party, if it is to be effective, must hold together.
It is no use electing a lot of Conservative or other
Members of Parliament unless they are prepared to
support a Government of their own colour.   No
doubt in past days when Burke wrote—or even a
good deal later—Members of Parliament were expected to maintain broadly the principles they advocated at the hustings, but to use their own judgment
as to how they should vote on particular issues, irrespective of the views and proposals of the Government of the day.   Wilberforce, for instance, was in
general a Tory and a supporter of Pitt.   But he did
not hesitate to vote against him, even on very crucial

questions such as that of Melville's impeachment,
where he thought Pitt wrong ; and his Yorkshire
constituents remained faithful to him in spite of
desperate attacks by official Whigs and Tories, backed
by enormous funds. Much later, instances of a
similar attitude may be found. Indeed until the
middle of the nineteenth century, the charge of
undue subservience to Party leaders was a more
damning accusation than that of Party disloyalty.
Since then the opposite opinion has steadily gained
ground. Party discipline and Party loyalty are the
officially-prized qualities. Party organisation in
Parliament has become more rigid and is in closer
connection with the organisation in the country. To
the directors of the Party fight a man who thinks
and acts for himself is a doubtful asset, and if he
quarrels with the Whips in the House his electoral
caucus will probably become troublesome. This is
natural enough, and in a degree respectable. It is
the possession and wielding of executive powers of
government that matter most. Legislation, though
a great outcry is made about it, is a clumsy weapon.
Administration is a handier and more powerful instrument. A Strafford-like direction of the administrative machinery can accomplish much more whether
in a reactionary or a revolutionary sense than any
mere law-making. No wonder then that the great
struggle is to bring into power and keep them there
Ministers who will apply the principles of the Party,
whatever they may be, and consequently only those

who can be trusted to vote " straight " are wanted as electoral candidates.

That is the Party reasoning and it is sound enough. The Party system is necessary if there is to be a stable Government carrying out the policy approved by the majority of the electors. That is indubitably true. A House of Commons in which each Member voted on every question, on what seemed to him the merits of that question alone, would mean that no Administration would be sure of carrying its policy into effect. Something like a paralysis of Government would result. As the sentry in *Iolanthe* sings :

> " The prospect of a lot
> Of dull M.P.'s in close proximity
> All thinking for themselves is what
> No man can face with equanimity."

And yet for the advantage of avoiding this danger the price must be paid, as it must for all other advantages. But it must not be too high. If M.P.'s are never to think for themselves, unless they are *very* dull, they may easily become dishonest. For it is unfortunately a law of human nature, that honest and intelligent men will think for themselves and arrive at various conclusions. If you want intelligent men to govern the country, Members of Parliament must be allowed liberty of thought and a certain amount of liberty of action. How much freedom can be conceded to the supporters of a Government without seriously impairing its efficiency is a difficult question.

In any case the true facts should be faced and acknow-
ledged.   The present conventions of Parliamentary
debate too often conceal the truth.   A Ministerialist,
who gets up in the House of Commons and says that
though he wholly disagrees with some Government
proposal he is going to vote for it rather than imperil
the Government, is usually greeted with howls of
derision.   He is conventionally assumed to be either
a cynic or a coward.   If, therefore, he is an ordinary
man, he makes an insincere speech pretending to
have been converted by arguments which in truth
he despises—and is heartily cheered.   That is due
to our national habit of pretending that a state of
things still exists which has in fact passed away.   A
hundred and twenty years ago in Wilberforce's day,
it would have been absurd for him to have voted
" against his conscience " as it is called.   At that
time no Government ever thought of resigning or
dissolving unless it was clear that it had lost the
confidence of the House.   Pitt did not resign over
the Melville division.   On the other hand Addington
did resign when a number of divisions had shown
that his Parliamentary support was slipping away,
though he was never actually beaten.   Generally
speaking, therefore, a Member could, at that date,
vote as he pleased without having to consider the
indirect result of his action on the existence of the
Government.   For many years now the system has
become different.   Almost every division on a
Government proposal is treated as a question of

confidence, and if the Government is defeated, even if it does not actually resign, its prestige and authority are more or less seriously shaken. That seems to me an unfortunate development of our constitutional system, due partly to the growing power of the bureaucracy which desires to force through Parliament every detail of its original proposals, partly to the idleness of electors who, rather than make up their minds as to the merits of each proposal, prefer to require their representative always to vote with his Party. Be this as it may, the result is that members of the majority can rarely vote according to what they regard as the merits of the question, if that happens to be contrary to the Government view, without running the risk of a Parliamentary crisis. If this were freely and openly recognised it would not perhaps matter. But as things stand the whole of each debate is conducted on a false footing. The House is supposed to be going to decide between the arguments for two opposing views of the question, when it may well be that a considerable number of members intend to vote in the Government lobby, not because they think Ministers right on the particular question raised, but because they think that a Government defeat will do more harm to the country than a wrong decision of that issue.

It is true that such dissidents are not altogether without a remedy. They can indulge in the practice I have heard described as " damning about the lobbies." They can, and do, tell the Chief Whip exactly what they think about the Government policy and threaten terrible, if somewhat nebulous, consequences if something is not done about it. They may even seek an interview with the leader of the Party, and with many expressions of loyalty and devotion explain to him that he is leading the country, and worse still the Party, to destruction ! All these alleviations are recognised as legitimate and proper, though wearing to the officials involved. A less admirable method of reprisals is to confide in the Lobby correspondent of an opposition paper, or if the worst comes to the worst, to go home to dinner without voting !

No one can regard this state of things as satisfactory. It is bad for the public life of the country that Members of the House of Commons should be continually placed in this equivocal and humiliating position. It must destroy the vitality of the House of Commons, and on the reputation of that House the whole constitution stands. Those of us who can remember the debates on the first Home Rule Bill will appreciate how much greater was the interest then taken in Parliamentary debates. The speeches of the protagonists, Mr. Chamberlain and Mr. Gladstone, were reported verbatim in all the more important newspapers and were read with deep attention by many thousands of their fellow-countrymen. Why ? Not only because they were great examples of argument and rhetoric ; but because they were political events of the first importance. The decision of the House of Commons was in doubt.   Up till the day before the division, good judges believed Mr. Gladstone would win.   Members were actually listening to the speeches because they wished to give a right decision on a momentous issue.   And because they listened, the country listened too.

If we want to keep alive the authority of Parliament we must preserve the reality of its debates.   To do that we must either allow Members to vote as they please on all, except a very few, vital questions— such as direct votes of censure or the Second Readings of First-Class Government Bills—or, if the opposite custom is now so hardened as to make such a change impossible, then to let them say quite frankly that they are voting, not on the merits of the question, but in support of the Government.

These difficulties are naturally less acute in the case of a Member of a Party in Opposition.   A vote by him against his Party will not cause a crisis.   The worst that can happen is that he may strengthen the Government of the day.   Even so, a man who votes often in such a way will not be popular.   He may find himself rejected as the Party candidate at the next election.   In any case he can scarcely hope for assistance from the Party funds.   Every year the bonds of Party discipline are drawn tighter.   Every year the standard of Party loyalty grows higher.   In a few years' time independence in Opposition may be as difficult as it is now for a Ministerialist.   I wish I could think that the change will make for a better and more public-spirited House of Commons. I am afraid the opposite result is far more probable, and I venture to press the importance of encouraging, by all means in our power, individuality and a reasonable degree of independence amongst our legislators.

There remains the very grave problem, which must from time to time arise, of when a Member ought to vote against his Party even at the cost of a change of Government. It is a problem that arises in other cases in a still more acute form. When should a Member of the Cabinet resign ? In his case the Party bond is absolutely rigid. For a century or more every Cabinet Minister has accepted responsibility for every act of the Government—even though in these days of large Cabinets and growing complication of the administrative machine, he may not have been as fully consulted as he has a right to be. He may perhaps be able to avoid expressly defending actions of which he disapproves. But as long as he is a Member of the Government, he is absolutely precluded by constitutional custom from opposing by speech and still more by vote any Government proceeding. If he wishes to differ he must resign.

When should he do so ? The problem is not an easy one in itself. A Minister may find himself in warm agreement with his colleagues on every point, except one. But that point may, in his opinion, touch the vital interests of his country. If he accepts responsibility for the policy of the Government in this matter, and it turns out as badly as he fears, he may be responsible for a serious national misfortune. And yet if he resigns he may not improbably hasten the return to power of the Opposition whose policy on other matters may be not less likely to injure British interests. Evidently he will have to choose the least of the evils presented to him. If the issue is really vital he will do well to resign. For if he remains he is directly responsible for the consequences to his country. Whereas if he resigns, at the worst he only contributes one of many factors in the defeat of his Party, for which the House of Commons or the electorate are mainly responsible. Still the retiring Minister must be very certain that the question in debate between him and his colleagues is in truth as important as he thinks it. It is very easy for a man of decided views or impatient temper to deceive himself in such a matter. Resignation is not a trivial thing. Nor for that matter is a vote against his Party by a Member of the House of Commons or even an elector. Party co-operation is essential to the Government of the country, and in those countries where it is lightly esteemed the result is a feeble executive, short-lived Governments without the authority necessary to control the clashing interests of their fellow-citizens or to impose on external Powers respect for the essential requirements of national existence and prosperity. Ministers and Members of the House of Commons must doubtless be on their guard lest the personal disadvantages of a breach with their Party should tempt them into what our Puritan forefathers would have called " weak compliances." It is equally true that a man who elevates every difference of opinion into a question of vital principle will show that he fails to appreciate that a large degree of Party solidarity is essential for the success of Parliamentary Government.

These considerations may be modified if, as sometimes happens, there is one question which dominates the political arena. During the world war for instance, not only were party politics in abeyance, but it was very generally felt that almost the only thing that would justify an individual in opposing the Government of the day was a conviction that it was taking some course which might imperil victory. That was an extreme case. But there have been political issues of immeasurably less importance which have yet occupied men's minds so exclusively as to require all in public life, great or small, to take their stand on the one side or the other, irrespective of other political considerations. The long drawn-out struggle over the franchise was, I suppose, one such question, at any rate in some of its phases. Home Rule was another. Free Trade perhaps a third. On occasions of this kind the public lays aside all ordinary Party predilections until as it were a plebiscite on the burning question of the day has been taken, and until that has been done Ministers and Members of the House of Commons are more or less freed from their Party loyalty, or rather acceptance or rejection of the proposal before the country becomes the only test of Party allegiance. On such occasions, all other feelings and opinions must give way to the one dominating issue.

Another circumstance may gravely affect Party adherence in a different way. A man may have publicly pledged himself to a particular opinion so definitely as to make it dishonourable for him to become responsible for a contrary policy. The leading case on the subject is that of Sir Robert Peel and the Corn Laws. As is well known he and his Party fought the 1841 election largely on Protection. He and they were pledged as deeply as it was possible to be against the repeal of the Corn Laws. When, therefore, he became convinced that repeal was necessary he resigned. So far all are agreed that he acted rightly. But when it appeared that no alternative Government could easily be formed, he returned to office in order to carry the policy which he had been elected to oppose. Approval of his course in so doing has been by no means unanimous. No one doubts his personal integrity in the matter. But some have thought that the obligation of his pledges was paramount. It is probably true that Sir Robert alone could have carried repeal. Certainly his parliamentary and administrative ability were pre-eminent. Nor is it to be doubted that he believed that without repeal the country would be in serious difficulties if not danger. Nevertheless many will hold that the reputation for trustworthiness of public men is of such overwhelming importance that all other considerations must give way to its maintenance. Another Conservative Minister in somewhat similar circumstances took a different view of his duty from that adopted by Sir Robert Peel. In 1866 the Liberal Government was defeated on a proposal to extend the franchise and a Conservative Government under Lord Derby and Mr. Disraeli took office. When they came to deal with the franchise question, the majority of the new Cabinet adopted proposals which were in their consequences more advanced than those of the Government they had replaced. Thereupon three members of the Cabinet, Lord Salisbury, Lord Carnarvon, and General Peel, resigned office rather than unsay in office what they had urged in Opposition. The Tory Government after an uneasy existence of some months was decisively defeated at the polls in 1868. It cannot be doubted that Lord Salisbury's action in 1867 contributed to the defeat in 1868 of the Government with which he was mainly in agreement. Nor will many people now think that he was right in his fears of the consequences of the 1867 Reform Act. Nevertheless I am convinced that he and his colleagues were right in resigning. Distrust of politicians is one of the great dangers of Parliamentary Government. It is very easily aroused. For reasons to which I have already adverted a Minister or a Member of the House of

Commons is frequently forced to support policies with which he is not altogether in agreement, and the man in the street is prone to believe that such action, which may in fact have been based on the highest motives, was dictated by the most sordid self-interest. That is unavoidable ; but it makes it all the more important that where a man has entered into express personal obligations he should be meticulous in their discharge. Whatever then may be thought of the very difficult and complicated case of Sir Robert Peel and the Corn Laws, it may safely be laid down as a general rule that if a man has given an express pledge as to his future political action he must not take advantage of any public position given to him, in consequence of that pledge, to carry out a policy inconsistent with it, however much he may persuade himself that public interest so requires.

It is very easy to deceive oneself in such matters. Reasons of State have too often been made the excuse for dirty or dishonourable actions. The pages of history are littered with instances of the kind, from the false promises of safety by which treacherous barbarians have induced garrisons to surrender and be massacred, down to the cynical subtleties of a Machiavelli or the shameless tergiversations of a Thurlow. Where these arch deceivers have led the way, many much more innocent politicians have followed. The argument is so attractive. A great national crisis arises. Only one way out of danger appears to exist, which the Government of the day proposes to take. Unfortunately some of the Ministers or their supporters are deeply pledged against it. If they insist on abiding by their pledges a ministerial crisis may arise—possibly a change of government with all its unforseeable complications. Are mere questions of personal consistency or even of personal honour to outweigh the safety of the country ? So runs the misleading suggestion. But the answer is clear. For a public man to break his word is an evil, both serious and certain. It cuts at the root of that confidence between man and man without which no government, certainly no democratic government, is possible. Public honour is vital to the State, and honour cannot be " rooted in dishonour." As to matters of State policy no such certainty exists. Every day the confident predictions of the wisest observers of political affairs are falsified ; and indeed in nine cases out of ten the supposed reasons of State turn out to be the figment of partisan excitement or even personal ambition. I remember when I was a young man reading in one of the Vailima letters of Robert Louis Stevenson a phrase which struck me then as expressing the real gist of the matter. He says :

" 'Tis easy to say that the public duty should brush aside these little considerations of personal dignity ; so it is that politicians begin, and in a month you will find them rat, and flatter and intrigue with brows of brass. I am rather of the old view that a man's first duty is to these little laws ; the big he does not, he never will, understand."

The longer I live the more certain I am that this is the only rule to follow.

What then are we to say of the Party system as a whole ?   Just this, that it is a means and a legitimate means to an end.   Without it Parliamentary Government cannot be effectively carried on ; there can be no stability, no vigorous executive, no fixed policy. But it must never be allowed to become an end in itself, and it must be based on a real foundation.   It must correspond with definite political ideas.   As soon as it ceases to do that it becomes an " organised hypocrisy."   We have seen in our own history and in that of other countries periods when parties seemed merely to exist in order to keep certain politicians in place.   Such was the combination of Fox and Burke with North in 1783.   Till they took office together they had been the bitterest of opponents. A year before Fox became the political ally of North he had told the House of Commons that " from the moment he should make any terms with one of them (the Ministers) he would rest satisfied to be called the most infamous of mankind.   He could not for an instant think of a coalition with such men who, in every public and private transaction as Ministers, had shown themselves void of every principle of honour and honesty.   In the hands of such men he would not trust his honour for a minute."   Burke had been scarcely less violent.   When therefore the two joined with the man they had denounced, not in order to carry through some great object of public policy on which they were agreed but merely to secure office, their King and country drove them from power and never forgave them. It is true that on the death of Pitt in the crisis of the French war, Fox was again in office for the last few months of his life, but that can scarcely be regarded as any modification of the verdict which his fellow-countrymen had pronounced upon him twenty-two years before.

It was from this unhappy experiment that the British distrust of Coalitions may be said to have sprung. It inspired Wilberforce to declare that " Coalitions are odious things, and lead to the dissolution of all principle and the loss of all credit in public men." And yet there is nothing more intrinsically objectionable in a combination of parties than in a combination of individuals to form a party, provided that in each case the purpose of the combination is to carry out some paramount object of policy. There have been many such Coalitions : the Coalition under Lord Aberdeen, the Unionist Coalition formed to defeat Home Rule, and the various Coalition Ministries under which the late War was carried to a successful conclusion. In each case men of different parties sunk minor differences in order to ward off what they considered to be a great national danger. That is perfectly legitimate and even admirable. All political co-operation, if it is to be more than fleeting, must involve a certain amount of compromise. In that sense every Party is more or less of a Coalition, for it contains and must

contain individuals and groups differing very considerably from one another, but kept together in
order to carry out certain larger policies on which
they are agreed. No one with any sense believes
that all the Members of a Party always think alike on
all questions. And the same is of course true of
Cabinets. By the convention already described,
Cabinets are supposed to be unanimous. In a sense
they are, since they are all agreed to act together. But
that is, and must be, frequently the limit of their
agreement. I have sat in four Cabinets and have
observed in all of them repeated occasions where the
Ministers have differed decidedly, though not so
fundamentally as to justify resignation. I do not
only mean that they have begun by differing and then
as the result of discussion have arrived at agreement.
That, of course, continually occurs. But in a certain
number of cases they have remained of their diverse
opinions, and have nevertheless consented to common
action as a less evil than a breach in the Government.
They have, in fact, agreed to differ. And this must
necessarily be so with fifteen or twenty reasonably
intelligent men who think for themselves. All that
we can reasonably claim is that in these known conditions the conventional protestations of unanimity
might with advantage be couched in somewhat less
decisive terms. The vital thing is not that there
should be no differences of opinion, but that the
Cabinet or the Party or the Coalition should be based
on a body of agreed principles. That is the key

to the difference between a healthy and an unhealthy Party system. It is reasonable and right that an elector should vote for the Party or the colour to which he and his have been traditionally attached, provided he still thinks that on the whole the interests of the country are safer in that Party's hands. But if he goes further and votes blue or buff, or red or green, without reference to his country's interest, and merely desiring to see the side with which he is connected win, as if it were a football or cricket match, then he is betraying his trust and is unworthy of the franchise which has been entrusted to him. So it is reasonable and right for a Member of Parliament to think carefully before he votes against his Party. He must reflect on the great importance of avoiding political crises; of the dangers of weak governments; of the impossibility of always getting your own way in politics as in other sublunary matters. But if, after weighing all that, he decides not only that the Government are, in the particular case, wrong, which must frequently happen to mortal men, but that the course which they are pursuing is fraught with danger to the prosperity or the existence of the country or is inconsistent with the pledges of himself and his Party, then let the consequences be what they may, he must vote against all the blandishments of the Party Whips and the threats of the Party caucus. The same rule holds with a Minister. He is certainly not to resign merely because he cannot agree with the majority of his colleagues on every question. Such a course, if it became customary, would make Cabinet Government impossible.   On the contrary, if after exhausting all means of reaching agreement he is still unable to assent to the policy proposed, he should consider first whether the matter is of first-rate importance, next whether there is not some means of postponing the issue, and lastly whether the adoption of the policy in question or a change of Government—for any resignation may produce and must contribute to such a consequence—is the greater evil ; and it is only after a full consideration of all these questions that resignation can be justified, subject to the one qualification that nothing must be done which is inconsistent with personal honour.   For, as I have already said, the one essential thing is to preserve the public confidence in the honour of statesmen and politicians.   Without that confidence Parliamentary Government cannot be carried on.   Nay, the Party system itself must become rotten and decayed.   Sixty years ago a great authority wrote :

" There is no blindness so unaccountable as the blindness of some British statesmen to the political value of a character.   Living only in and for the House of Commons, moving in an atmosphere of intrigue, accustomed to look upon oratory as a mode of angling for political support and on political professions as only baits of more or less attractiveness, they acquire a very peculiar code of ethics, and they are liable to lose sight of the fact that there is a stiffer and less corrupted morality out of doors.   They not only come to forget what is right, but they forget there is anyone who knows it."

Is that an overstatement? Some may think so. And yet does it not convey a needed warning? a warning of consequences which have followed the abuse of Party politics in other times, and unless we take care may ensue in our own. The temptation to a politician to acquire a " very peculiar code of ethics " is chronic. It is certainly not less now than heretofore. Are we all doing our part to maintain the " stiffer " and " less corrupted " out-of-door morality which strengthens him to resist the temptation? Do we require our Parliamentary representatives and public men to do the best that is in them? Or do we throw our weight on the other side and incite them to be not better but rather worse than other men, less conscientious, less courageous, less honest? It is of the essence of a self-governing community that all enfranchised citizens should take their part in public life. No one has a right to stand aside. No one has a right to put his conscience in another's keeping. His and his alone is the responsibility for what he does or does not do, for what he says or does not say in national affairs. He must not expect perfection.

I have criticised the Party system. But there it is and it is the only available instrument of government. If it has its defects it has its great merits. The merging of the individual in corporate life, be it that of the Party or of the State, calls for devotion and self-sacrifice. It brings out great qualities—some of the greatest in human nature.

We must be vigilant lest party develops into faction with all the attendant evils of hypocrisy and corruption. But vigilance must not be an excuse for timidity or self-indulgence. There is much to be done, many causes to be served. Selfishness, arrogance, cruelty still flourish in the world. Envy, hatred, and all uncharitableness still produce their evil fruits. Vice and poverty at home, suspicion and hostility abroad, summon us to political activity. Let us by all means purify our Party politics. But do not let us from prudery or Pharisaism or idleness shrink from the tasks which our common citizenship has laid upon us.

III

CONSERVATISM AND PEACE (I)

(1924)

A FRIEND of mine told me the other day that he had been to a gathering of young Conservatives which had been addressed by a distinguished Conservative statesman. They had been adjured to show more enthusiasm for " the Cause." " Look at the Labour party," said the speaker : " look at their untiring energy, their belief in the Labour policy, their ceaseless propaganda. No wonder they have made so much way. We must imitate them and work as hard as they do, or harder. Then the success of Conservative policy will be assured." " Unfortunately," said my friend, " we were not told what was the cause for which we were to fight. What is Conservatism ? What are Conservative principles ? What is the Conservative creed ? " Urgent searching questions ! It is as a contribution towards their answer that the following pages have been written.

Conservatism as a party creed was first promulgated by Sir Robert Peel in 1835. It was an expedient devised to meet a difficult parliamentary situation. The Tory party had been disastrously defeated as a result of the great Reform Bill. And yet the Whigs, apparently the victors, were many of them anxious and dissatisfied. They did not know what would happen next, they had no desire for far-reaching change, and they were at least as terrified of Revolution as the Tories. To a " great member of Parliament " like Peel the political game to be played was obvious. The moderate Whigs must be induced to support the Tories as the only way to avoid Revolution. For this purpose a new policy was necessary, as anodyne and colourless as possible, to which all moderate men might assent. Such a policy could hardly be anything but negative. To advocate any positive action might frighten away political recruits. Far better play a waiting game until the country became disgusted with the Radicals and fled for refuge and relief to the new Conservative party.

To Disraeli and his Young England friends the plan seemed deplorable. It is described in *Coningsby* as " an attempt to construct a party without principles," the inevitable consequence of which was " Political Infidelity."

" ' Conservatism '," he says, " assumes in theory that everything established should be maintained ; but adopts in practice that everything that is established is indefensible. To reconcile this theory and this practice, they produce what they call the best bargain ; some arrangement which has no principle and no purpose except to obtain a temporary lull of agitation, until the mind of the Conservatives, without a guide and without an aim, distracted, tempted and bewildered, is prepared for another arrangement, equally statesmanlike with the preceding one."

Nevertheless, in the hands of that brilliant parliamentary tactician, Sir Robert Peel, Conservatism produced some striking immediate successes. Five years after the Reform Bill the Conservative Opposition in the House of Commons had become almost as numerous as the Ministerialists, and by 1841 there was a comfortable Conservative majority. True, this was shattered by the Fiscal controversy, and the Conservatives remained in a minority for thirty years. But that disaster was not put down to Conservatism, which more and more established itself as the party creed. Even when Disraeli became the leader of the party he did little or nothing to replace it by something more inspiring. In consequence, for nearly a generation the Conservative forces were engaged in fighting a series of rearguard actions, always being driven from the positions they occupied, and never putting forward any positive alternative to the policy of their opponents. Perhaps it was inevitable. But the fact remains that so long as the Conservative policy was purely negative, it failed. Not only did the Conservatives never hold office except for a few months at a time by the sufferance of their opponents, but in almost every case they were unable to preserve what they were fighting for. There were controversies over the Church, over the Army, over Education. On all these questions, whether we think the Conservative party right or wrong, one thing is clear, that it was unsuccessful. The same is true of its fiscal policy whether in resistance to Free Trade or the Death Duties. And as regards the chief political issue of the century, Reform, it only escaped repeated defeat by retiring so rapidly that the innovating forces were unable to keep up with it.

All this does not necessarily mean that " Conservatism " was wrong. It may have been that, in the circumstances, the only possible policy was to say No to all the Whig and Radical proposals. There may have been no alternative policy available. But whether that be so or not, the event showed that a purely negative policy makes no popular appeal and should therefore only be resorted to by a political party if no other course is open to it consistent with its principles. Positive examples will perhaps make the contention clearer. Take Irish Land. So long as the Conservative party confined itself to resisting Gladstone's Irish Land Policy it failed completely. Act after Act was passed taking the property of the landlord piece by piece and giving it to the tenant. The Land Acts of 1870 and of 1881, the Arrears Act of 1882, and all the smaller amending Acts, followed one another in regular succession in spite of vehement Conservative protests of a strictly negative character. Then Land Purchase as an alternative policy came on the scene. It was adopted by both parties interested as a just solution of their difficulties, and the piecemeal confiscation of the landowners' property came to an end.

Or take the Disestablishment of the Church in Ireland, Wales, and England. Had the Conservative party adopted a policy of concurrent endowment of the religious bodies in Ireland, the Irish Establishment and some part of the Endowment might have been saved. In fact, blind and uncompromising resistance was preferred in spite of the glaring disproportion of endowment to service which actually existed in that country. The result was complete defeat. Similarly with the Welsh Church, nothing was done to meet the really strong sentiment for a National Church until too late. On the other hand, the demand for the Disestablishment of the Church in England has almost died away. Why? Because English Churchmen were not contented with a rejection of the " Liberationist " proposals. They advocated and carried through a liberationist policy of their own, reforming abuses and giving to the Church such a measure of self-government as removed all genuine ground for the contention that it was the slave of the State. Or take Home Rule. We have reached, it may be, a settlement of the Irish question ; it may be only a pause in its development. We all hope the present system will be durable, and will succeed. But two things are quite clear about it. In the first place, it means the complete reversal of the Unionist policy for which so many famous statesmen of the last generation did so much. And in the second, no one can contemplate the means by which the settlement was brought about, the crimes of its

Irish advocates, the lawlessness of their attempted repression, the disregard of loyalist interests, without profound misgivings as to what will be the ultimate result.   How much better it would have been had it been possible to arrive at some alternate settlement earlier by the adoption either of Mr. Chamberlain's four council suggestion or some other similar plan ! In any case, here, too, the Unionist policy, so far as it was a purely negative policy, failed.

It may be said that in the case of Home Rule the Unionist policy very nearly succeeded.   I believe that is true.   But for the Conservative rout of 1905-6, which had nothing to do with Ireland, there certainly seemed good ground for the opinion that the agitation for Home Rule was dying away.   The Liberal party felt the cause to be so hopeless that they pledged themselves in the election not to attempt to carry Home Rule in the Parliament then to be elected. There is, too, the often quoted declaration of Mr. Birrell a year later, that Ireland had never been so peaceful or so prosperous for centuries.   But these results were largely due to the fact that the Unionist policy was not purely negative.   With the rejection of Home Rule had gone a whole series of constructive measures designed to cure Irish discontent.   The Land Purchase policy had settled the land question. The grant of County Councils had done something to satisfy the demand for self-government.   Considerable grants of money had been made to relieve distress, to remedy the deplorable conditions of agricultural housing, and to carry out various public works and improvements.

Further, if English and, to some extent, Scottish opinion stood firmly in support of the Unionist position for many years as they did, it was largely because the resistance to Home Rule was part of the great wave of Imperialist feeling which was as far as possible from being Conservative in the narrow sense. It was only when Imperialism had suffered from its connection first with the Boer War, or, rather, with the cold fit which inevitably followed that war like all other wars, and secondly, with the proposal to put a tax on corn and meat, that a Home Rule majority was obtained in Parliament. With the weakening of the Imperialist bulwark to Unionism, little was left except the exclusively negative attitude to Home Rule which was as usual unable to secure popular endorsement.

It is not pretended that the foregoing analysis is complete. Political victory does not always attend the advocacy of a constructive programme. Nor is an attitude of negation always followed by political defeat. In certain moods of the electorate Conservatism, or, to give it a more recent name, Tranquillity, is popular. Exhausted by the restlessness of Gladstone's 1868 administration, the electors were glad to establish a Disraeli government in 1874 which promised chiefly repose and sanitation. So, too, the Conservative domination from 1886 to 1905 was mainly due to opposition to Home Rule, though, as has already been indicated, this did not entirely depend on negative considerations. Conversely, the Unionist disaster of 1906 was produced, in part at least, by the unpopularity of the positive proposals for Tariff Reform. But in both the latter cases there was a disturbing cause of great power, namely, party disunion. It was the defection of the Liberal Unionists in 1886 that delayed Home Rule for a generation, and the similar revolt of the Unionist Free Traders in 1904 that smashed Tariff Reform. Even so, Home Rule is now law, and some people believe that Tariff Reform will also, sooner or later, be adopted.

Whether that proves to be so or not, the argument here put forward remains unaffected, for no one will say that the attitude of the Free Trade parties has been exclusively negative.

On the whole, then, Disraeli's judgment may be accepted, that what he called " Political Infidelity," the attitude of Goethe's Mephistopheles *der stets verneint*, has very small prospect of political success, at any rate in opposition to proposals for dealing with an admitted evil. It may, no doubt, be true that evils exist for which there is no remedy, and that ill-considered attempts to put them right will only do more harm than good. But it is also true that those are most likely to assent to this proposition who are not themselves exposed to the evils in question. And it is certain that passive acquiescence in hardship or suffering affecting large masses of the population is not an attitude that is likely to prove very inspiring to the average elector.

It does not follow from these considerations that, once it is conceded that conditions of life for this or that section of our fellow-countrymen are unsatisfactory, we ought to accept the first nostrum that is put forward as a cure. That would be a defiance of all Conservative principle which, whatever else it means, certainly implies care and caution in advocating change. No one can contemplate for a moment the immense complexity of modern civilisation without realising the danger of sudden or violent alterations, however plausible they may at first sight appear. Scarcely a Bill is framed by Parliament which has not some remote or unexpected results. In all the long and elaborate debates on Mr. Lloyd George's land taxes I do not think it was once pointed out that their chief effect would be to hold up the building of houses for the working classes. Few people realised that the principal result of the Merchandise Marks Act would be to promote the sale of certain kinds of foreign-made goods ; and it was equally unforeseen that the establishment of a licensing system for the purpose of regulating the liquor traffic would confer upon the licence holders a vested interest which has been one of the chief obstacles to temperance reform ever since.

But though legislation and, indeed, State action of any kind is much too clumsy an instrument to be used without great caution, we ought to be very chary

of rejecting out of hand a remedy brought forward
to meet a genuine grievance, unless we are prepared
to make an alternative proposal which we believe to
be superior. We may be driven to that course ; but
let us remember, if we are, that it is not at all likely
to be successful. Take Socialism, the great issue of
the present day. There is a school of political
speakers and writers who are urging us to concentrate
on the defeat of Socialism. By all means ; only let
us first know what we understand by Socialism, and
next let us consider very carefully what is the best
way of meeting it. Socialism, as preached nowadays,
has many gradations which fade into one another.
But two main lines of thought may be distinguished.
There are those Socialists who are chiefly anxious to
increase the power of the State. They are usually
against confiscation, and advocate, where necessary,
expropriation of individual owners of property on
fair terms. In contrast to this school are those who
disapprove in principle of private property and whose
main preoccupation is to get rid of it wherever they
can. If they admit at all the principle of compensation where property is " resumed " by the State,
it is only as a concession to human weakness. It
follows that the compensation given, if any, must be
on a very restricted scale. Conservatives, it may be
assumed, are opposed to both sets of proposals ; to
the first on the familiar grounds that State interference is deadening and oppressive, that it destroys
liberty and initiative, that it is very expensive and

leads to the corruption of public life ; and to the second, on all these grounds, and further because confiscation of private property would be immoral and would lead to the destruction of all confidence and security on which prosperity, and even society, is and must be based. The important question is, How can we most effectively convince the electorate of these truths ? Certainly not by mere denunciation and threatening the country with Bolshevism. It is quite useless to represent the leaders of the present Labour party as revolutionaries. It is equally foolish to treat all Socialists as substantially identical and to suggest, for example, that the nationalisation of railways is the first step towards Communism. I myself have always been opposed to nationalisation of railways. But many vigorous upholders of law and order, like Mr. Churchill for instance, have at times taken a different view. Nor should it be forgotten that the railways belong to the State in many of our dominions, in such conservative countries as Switzerland, pre-war Germany, and in some cases in France. We cannot even make much of our old friend the thin-end-of-the-wedge argument, for municipal tramways and gas, and electric and water supply concede the principle of public ownership for certain public services. All that can properly be said on the subject is that the economic arguments against State railways are stronger than those in their favour, and that the political objections to an enormous increase of State employers in a country governed by parliamentary institutions are very formidable. No sane member of Parliament would like to see great additions to the existing number of dockyard constituencies.

No doubt it is true that the moderate or Fabian Socialists have made common cause with men who really are out for quite different objects. The typical Fabian is a bureaucrat like Lord Olivier or Mr. Sidney Webb. He believes that officials are wiser and more competent than other men, and that the advantages of private enterprise are all moonshine, or worse. But his associate, the Marxian or the Communist, is quite another thing, and he it is who gives to the Labour movement much of its enthusiasm. The Glasgow black squad are formidable people. They are deeply in earnest and absolutely sincere. They are small in numbers, but they have the spirit of crusaders, and in a Parliament with a Labour majority they would constitute a serious danger to the country. And their strength is that the premises from which they argue are quite true. Take a man like Mr. Lansbury, for instance. He is hysterical and unbalanced, if you like. But he is transparently honest. He is deeply moved, as we all ought to be, by the shocking conditions in which great numbers of our fellow-men are living. Shameful housing conditions, overcrowded and insanitary dwellings; sweated labour, exploitation of the weak by the strong, of the poor by the rich; undeserved and demoralising unemployment; tyranny and injustice by bad employers ; unconscionable use of monopolies by certain urban landowners and others—all these things exist, and are a bitter reproach to our civilisation. True, these conditions are the exception and not the rule. But their existence gives to Socialist teaching just that moral fervour which the creed of its opponents is apt to lack. The Socialist orator—I am not now speaking of scientific Socialism, but of the popular street-corner brand—seizes on the existence of these evils and declares that they are the direct outcome of capitalism. If certain workers have to put up with dog-kennels instead of houses it is the fault partly of the landlord who exploits his local monopoly by demanding excessive rents, and partly of the employer who gives insufficient wages to provide proper housing. If vast numbers of unemployed, willing and anxious to work, are walking the streets, it is because capitalism requires a pool of workers from which to draw as may be required to enable profits to be earned and employers to live in luxury. If men and women are sweated and victimised it is because they are mere wage slaves compelled to accept the wages offered and to submit to the conditions of labour imposed by autocratic masters. And then follows the inevitable peroration describing the senseless and wicked extravagance of the idle rich in contrast to the hardship and suffering meted out to the only true producers of wealth, the working classes.

All this is grossly exaggerated, and in some respects

actually false. But it is genuinely believed. Nor
can it be displaced by elaborate arguments to prove
that it is in part inevitable and for the rest would be
made worse and not better by Socialism. Something
more than that is needed. If it could be shown that
our present industrial system on the whole worked
pretty well and without friction, it might be possible
to induce the wage-earners to put up with exceptional
cases of hardship. But that, unfortunately, cannot
be maintained. Every day we read in the paper of
some new and serious industrial trouble. As soon
as a railway dispute is settled we are plunged into a
dock strike. With difficulty the dockers are appeased
and we are faced with a stoppage in the mines. And
besides these industrial pitched battles there are continually occurring minor combats and skirmishes,
each of which inflicts injury to our economic life and
has to be paid for sooner or later in poverty and unemployment. Nor is it true that in these controversies the workers are always wrong. To an outside
observer the blame seems pretty equally divided
between employers and employed. Or rather, is
it not the real fact that the system is at fault? To
that extent it seems to me the Socialists are right.
Our present industrial mechanism is out of gear.
Somehow or another we have got into a condition in
which employers and employed look upon themselves
as being in opposite camps. Each combatant seems
to believe that the other is striving to deprive him of
his legitimate reward and that the only way of getting

his rights is to fight for them. Instead of devoting their whole energies to increase production and diminish waste, a great part of their efforts are absorbed in this senseless warfare.[1]

Does not this state of things give the Conservative Party a great opportunity ? Socialism, even at its face value, has no immediate remedy to offer. Assuming its case to be true, some day many years hence by the complete transformation of the whole industrial system and the suppression of all private enterprise it is possible that the contest between employers and employed may be stopped, though the actual examples of public employment in the Post Office and elsewhere are not very encouraging. Pending the adoption of the complete Socialist system Socialists, as such, can do nothing. Conservatism is not so powerless. For no political principle should Conservatives be more enthusiastic than for that of unity. It is the very basis of all stability. Just as the fighting Socialists are driven to preach class consciousness and class warfare in order to bring about the destruction of the established order, so the party of stability must work with all their strength for unity. If that can be achieved there is no fear of revolution or even unrest. And in particular the maddening and dangerous divisions in the industrial world would be ended. How can it be done ?

[1] This was truer in 1924 than it is now. But even now it is fundamentally accurate.

The main political evil of the day is suspicion.   It is so internationally, and it is so betwixt employers and employed at home.   It is that more than anything else which keeps the classes apart.   For ever the workman suspects that he is being cheated by his master, the employer believes that there is some unavowed motive for the demands of his employees. On the one side there is talk of agitators, on the other of greediness and tyranny.   There may be occasionally some truth in the charges and countercharges. But to an onlooker they seem, in nine cases out of ten, unfounded.   There is only one cure for this disease, and that is to bring the two sides into closer personal relations with one another, and, above all, for both sides to put all their cards on the table.

That is why Whitley councils, so far as they go, are such an excellent thing.   They do give an opportunity for talking things over.   But they do not go far enough.   They do not give to the workman the sense that he is personally interested in the success of the undertaking in which he is engaged.   That, too, is where piecework fails.   It gives an incentive to individual exertion, but it does no more.   It makes no appeal to corporate feeling, *esprit de corps*, call it what you will, which experience shows is one of the most powerful and beneficent of human motives. Let me give an example.

During the War, when wages generally were rising, the manager of a large gas company gave notice that after a certain date the wages of their employees would be raised.   Whereupon the workmen made representations that the proposal was ill-advised, since the profits of the company could not stand the expense, and for some weeks the rise was postponed, until the increase in the cost of living made it inevitable.   In that company complete solidarity had been obtained between employers and employed, and the reason was that it was and is worked on co-partnership principles. Under the system in force every regular workman has, in addition to his wages, a share in the profits calculated on the basis of his wages ; he is encouraged to invest in the capital of the company, and in practice does so ; and he and his fellows elect one-third of the board of directors.   What has been the result ? Since co-partnership was adopted, some forty years ago, there has not been a single strike, though up to that date the works were in a constant condition of unrest, and the company's trading results will compare favourably with those of any similar undertaking.

I know it is said that a gas company is in a special position, and that in a business of a different character the plan would not work.   The answer is that it has been tried with success in several other kinds of industry.   Indeed, it is my own belief that wherever co-partnership has been given a fair chance it has succeeded.   The difficulty is not that it fails when it is tried, but that it is not tried.   Militant trade-unionists distrust it because it is thought to weaken the solidarity of labour.   Socialists dislike it as bolstering up capitalism. Some employers disapprove of it as a new-fangled and troublesome arrangement. Others will have none of it because it may diminish their autocratic power in their own works. But I am confident that the great mass of workmen and a large majority of employers would welcome a serious effort to popularise and assist the adoption of the system.

In such a state of opinion wise political action may be of the greatest service. I do not advocate compulsory legislation or anything of that kind. The very essence of co-partnership is goodwill on both sides, and that is difficult if not impossible to secure by compulsion. But short of that, much might be done. There are certain difficulties caused by the Companies and Companies Clauses Acts which might be removed. Advantages might be offered to co-partnership undertakings when opportunity served. For instance, if wages boards were to be established it might be provided that if the employers and employed preferred to adopt an approved system of co-partnership they might do so. Above all, the Government Departments concerned might be instructed to promote co-partnership whenever possible. They might prepare model schemes for different industries—for there is no sealed pattern applicable to every industry alike. They might collect information as to experiments not only here but in other countries—not mere lists of cases where something like co-partnership or profit-sharing has been tried—but helpful facts showing what difficulties have been met with and how they have been overcome. Lastly, when serious disputes occurred and the mediation or advice of the Government was sought, the Department might suggest to the parties the establishment of co-partnership as the best way of avoiding future controversies.

I venture to claim that such a policy would be an instance of genuine Conservative reform. Not reactionary—for it follows the same direction as our political development. From one point of view, indeed, it may be described as a step towards the democratisation of industry. Still less is it revolutionary, for it aims at stability and domestic peace. Like peasant proprietorship of the land it is designed to broaden the economic basis of society. Nor is it the least of its merits that though the extremists of Labour and Capital alike reject it, it commands the sympathy and support of moderate men of all parties.

Doubtless many difficulties would remain, even if industrial suspicion were abolished. It is not pretended that any reform of the relations between employers and employed is a cure-all. There is housing, for instance—the apparently insurmountable difficulty of building sufficient houses for the working class at prices which will enable the tenants to pay an economic rent for the accommodation provided.[1]

[1] Since these words were written the energetic policy of Mr. Neville Chamberlain has effected a notable improvement. Much, of course, remains to be done in the direction of slum clearance, but, for the first time for many years, the actual supply of houses is beginning to approximate to the need.

The problem is urgent and dangerous. The conditions under which large numbers of our fellow-
citizens are housed are a scandal. They are an outrage on decency and morality which, if it is to
continue, must rouse such an outburst of justifiable
impatience as will compel some hasty solution. That
can only be found in eleemosynary building by
public authorities out of public funds. Unfortunately we have already started along that road. The
Coalition Government, rightly or wrongly, began the
system of using State money to erect houses which
should be let at rents bearing no relation to the cost
of construction, and it is now very difficult to break
away suddenly from that policy. But the precedent
is serious. State aid is apt to end in State provision,
as in the case of education, and unless we are careful
we shall find ourselves committed to the principle
that working-class housing ought to be provided rent
free out of the rates and taxes. And if houses why
not food, clothing, and other necessaries? All
parties object to doles of money as weakening the
self-respect of the recipient. By no one have they
been more unsparingly condemned than by the
present Minister of Labour. But State gifts in kind
are just as demoralising as doles of money—in some
ways more so, since their eleemosynary character is
more easily glossed over.

For the moment it is not possible to withdraw State
aid from housing. But Conservatives will desire to
see that course taken as soon as possible, both on the

general ground already indicated and because of the vast burden the opposite policy might eventually impose on our national finances. To re-establish housing on a sound economic basis the cost of building must be reduced or the tenants must be enabled to pay increased rents, and in both directions a better organisation of industry would help. For under an improved system, where all engaged, whether in the manufacture of building material or in the building itself, worked together single-mindedly for the success of their common object, production would go up, prices would come down, and at the same time working-class wages generally would be maintained, or even increased.

Unemployment, the other great social problem of the day, is in a different category. No doubt anything which added to our efficiency would tend to make it easier to sell our goods and thus to diminish unemployment. In that sense industrial reorganisation might be of service, just as tariff reformers believe that protection might help. But it seems unlikely that either in the one case or the other the effect would be very considerable. It is common ground that the present severe restriction of the labour market is mainly due to the poverty of our old customers, or perhaps more to the dislocation of the credit system on which modern commerce is built. No rapid cure for this disease can be looked for. The evil is too vast and its roots are too deep-seated. Nor can it be hoped that any moderate change of our existing machinery of production or exchange would produce much effect, and a violent change would certainly do more harm than good. All we can hope to do for the present is to apply palliatives as we have been doing. After all, it is better for the Treasury to run risks of losing money by not fully secured advances than to pay it away out and out in doles; and it is in every way better to keep men at work in their proper employment than to make grants to those who have become workless.

It is on this ground that the proposal to grant a bonus to arable farming may be properly defended, not so much because the numbers of the agricultural population ought to be maintained as because without some such assistance there is grave danger that many of those now so employed will be thrown out of work with a consequent aggravation of our unemployment difficulties. It may be said that if this is reasonable in the case of agriculture, why is it not equally reasonable in the case of other industries in a similar economic position, and there is great force in the observation. It certainly seems a most wasteful proceeding to levy large sums from the employers, the workmen, and the taxpayers, not to keep men in work but to pay them for being idle. In the present emergency, resulting from the War, it seems impossible to avoid this. But unemployment in a milder form is endemic. It recurs with heartrending regularity, and we have so accustomed ourselves to the alternation of booms and slumps that they are regarded as part of the order of nature.   In fact, they are nothing of the kind.   They are simply defects in our machinery of production, which ought not to be tolerated.   It would be far better if the State were to use its resources to limit the undue expansion as well as the restriction of business, and it should not pass the wit of man to devise means for doing so.   For instance, in some cases it might be possible to keep industries going in time of depression by the use of State credit, even if the effect of that were to place a limit on the extent of their recovery when the depression was over.

If a reliance on the principle of unity gives the best hope for the settlement of our domestic difficulties, it is equally applicable to external affairs.   Here we are in less disputatious country.   Every one accepts in principle the unity of the Empire, though there are differences as to the best method of achieving it.   So far as the self-governing dominions are concerned, the differences are, it is to be hoped, not very serious. Such as they are, they are concerned with the policy of preference.   Even here they are not so great as might be thought from the violence of the language sometimes used.   No one seriously advocates the imposition of duties in order to give a preference. On the other hand, most people would admit that if duties are imposed for other reasons it is reasonable to give a preference on them to the Dominions.   The question of what those duties should be is another one altogether, upon which there are no doubt very strong differences of opinion.

Apart from this question, the Conservative policy of the Empire has become the policy of all parties so far as the self-governing Dominions are concerned. No longer do we hear complacent talk of " cutting the painter." The old " little England " school is dead or, at the worst, survives in a few of those who belong to the reactionary section of the Liberal party. With regard to the rest of the Empire the questions raised are much more difficult. If the present Government[1] were to act on some of the statements of policy made by some of its members when they were in a position of greater freedom and less responsibility, the situation might become intensely serious. Fortunately, they seem to have short memories and docile dispositions. All that we need do at present is to make it as easy as possible for them to forget their old opinions.

In Foreign Policy there is also a large measure of agreement. The fantastic proposals to scrap the Versailles Treaty have been dropped. Nor can any exception be taken to the declarations by all parties in favour of the League of Nations. The League is the highest expression in international affairs of the principle of unity. It is based on the conception that by bringing the representatives of the nations together in a neutral atmosphere co-operation will be promoted and international disputes will be settled or

---

[1] The Labour Government of 1924.

mollified. So far its operations have been remarkably successful and its prestige and authority are steadily growing. It is to be wished that the Conservative party were more outspoken in its support. Of all sections of political opinion, they, both by tradition and reason, should be the warmest adherents of peace; for none have more to lose from the violence and national unrest caused by war. Nothing but war, so far as can be seen, would so dislocate society as to make Revolution possible in this country.

There is, however, one point in our foreign policy which in the near future may give rise to considerable discussion. Every one will agree that the great obstacle to the restoration of peace and to the revival of prosperity in Europe is the Franco-German difficulty or group of difficulties.[1] With regard to the Reparations side of it, nothing useful can be said till the expert committees have reported. But whatever their report, it is very unlikely that a settlement will be reached unless the even more important question of French security, or rather, French and German security, is also dealt with. The position is quite simple. Here are two nations who have been enemies for centuries. They have repeatedly invaded one another, and the invading forces have behaved as such forces usually do. Territory on their

[1] The Locarno Pact of 1925, and the subsequent entry of Germany into the League of Nations, have brought about a welcome change in Franco-German relations.

borders has changed hands more than once. National humiliation has been suffered and inflicted. At the present time the one that is numerically the weakest is victorious, and with the assistance of her allies has imposed terms that are bitterly resented by the other. A large party in Germany makes no secret of the fact that they hope for revenge, or, at the least, a forcible revision of the Treaty they have been compelled to accept. Can anybody wonder that in these circumstances it is the chief public preoccupation of every Frenchman and still more every Frenchwoman how they can protect their children, if not themselves, from future German attacks? If to some of us the French seemed unreasonable over Reparations, if they appeared to pursue a policy which made their payment so insistently demanded almost impossible, the explanation is to be found in the same cause. In principle, most Frenchmen will admit that unless Germany recover her prosperity she cannot be expected to make large foreign payments. But when suggestions are made which will in fact restore Germany's wealth, the vision of their enemy renewed in power and again a menace to their safety makes the same Frenchmen hastily reject anything which might lead to such a result. Meanwhile, the whole of Europe is kept anxious and unquiet until this great debate has been composed.

If, then, European reconstruction is to proceed and the foreign commerce on which our people so largely depend is to be revived, we must devise some means of appeasing French fears. The obvious way is to offer her an alliance against German aggression. That was the plan adopted in the tripartite pact between the United States, France, and ourselves, drawn up at Paris in 1919. Upon its rejection by America that proposal fell to the ground. A similar treaty was suggested by Mr. Lloyd George at Cannes, in 1922, confined to England and France. It was rather vague in its terms, and on that ground was in substance refused by M. Poincaré unless it was made much more specific. British opinion also declared against this proposal on the ground that it would tend to perpetuate the division of Europe into two groups, an opinion intensified by the conclusion of the Rapallo agreement a few months later between Russia and Germany. The result is that the Cannes proposals must be regarded as also definitely at an end. France, therefore, which abandoned her claim at Paris that the Rhine should be made her military frontier in return for the tripartite pact, has got neither the physical security of a natural obstacle to invasion nor the conventional security of a military alliance, and her anxiety for the future remains one of the great disturbing elements of the international situation. Meanwhile, the League of Nations has been approaching the problem from another angle. It is part of the League's duty, laid upon it by the treaties of peace, to try to devise some method for a general reduction of armaments. As the result of prolonged consideration, at the last meeting of the

Assembly a draft treaty was forwarded to the Governments of the world whereby, in return for measures of general disarmament to be agreed upon, the existing obligations laid upon members of the League to guarantee one another against aggression were to be made more definite and precise for all those who became parties to the suggested treaty. It is unnecessary here to go into the details of this plan. Its importance in this connection is that French opinion has accepted it as a satisfaction of their demand for security. It has further this advantage, that it offers to all who enter into the treaty an equal guarantee. If, therefore, Germany adhered to it, and it would be open to her to do so, she would be as much protected against possible French aggression as France would be against her. Along those lines a real solution seems possible. Any other plan must lead sooner or later to the re-creation of the group system in Europe, which was one of the main causes of the World War.

It is suggested that this scheme recognises the realities of the situation. It gives to France the security her people demand without creating an international position which experience has shown to be dangerous ; and it makes a general reduction of armaments possible, without which our national position may well become alarming. The recent Singapore incident shows the risk we run unless we have some coherent and well-thought-out policy on the subject. Whatever may be thought of the actual

merits of the Singapore controversy it is surely most
hazardous to defend the policy of the present Government on the ground that it is a " moral gesture "
towards disarmament. How far will that take us ?
Not apparently at present as far as refusing to replace
the five cruisers. But it is difficult to see why not.
Both measures were put forward by the highest
technical opinion as essential to the mobility and
efficiency of our Fleet. If it be sound policy to
encourage general disarmament by abandoning one
scheme, it is difficult to see the logical justification
for maintaining the other. In the absence of international agreement on the subject, piecemeal disarmament by the most pacific of the great powers,
ourselves, has no tendency towards permanent pacifi-
cation. We have already gone very far in that direction, as our experience in air armaments shows.
Some general policy is essential for our safety, and it
will be thoroughly in accordance with Conservative
tradition if the Conservative party are the authors
of it.

In Foreign affairs, then, no less than in domestic,
there is urgent need for a real Conservative policy
neither reactionary nor revolutionary, not merely a
reluctant and belated adoption of the measures
of our opponents, but offering a genuine remedy
for the distresses and difficulties of the times
along lines leading not to confusion but to
ordered progress. Let us remember the words
written some forty years ago by the states-

man [1] who led the Conservative forces to twenty years of victory :

" The object of our party is not and ought not to be simply to keep things as they are.   In the first place the enterprise is impossible.   In the next place there is much in our present mode of thought and action which it is highly undesirable to conserve. What we require is the administration of public affairs, whether in the executive or legislative department, in that spirit of the old constitution which held the nation together as a whole and levelled its united force at objects of national import instead of splitting it into a bundle of unfriendly and distrustful fragments."

That doctrine is at the root of the whole Conservative Creed, and upon it may well be founded a vital and vigorous Conservative Policy.

[1] Lord Salisbury.

IV

CONSERVATISM AND PEACE (II)

THERE is a legend fostered by the political adversaries of our Party that we are by tradition and conviction the Party of War. Nothing could be less true. Tories from Bolingbroke to Beaconsfield have been advocates of peace ; and Lord Beaconsfield's successor had, as I can personally testify, an almost fanatical hatred of war. Indeed, it so happens that of the four larger wars in which this country has been engaged since the Reform Bill of 1832, three were begun under definitely non-Conservative ministries, and for the fourth a Radical Unionist member of a Conservative administration was chiefly responsible.

Nor is this surprising. Whether we call ourselves Tories or Conservatives or Constitutionalists, the Party of the Right must necessarily stand for the two great principles of Stability and Unity ; and war is the enemy of both. Not only is it true that the great friend of Revolution is Want, and that Want is the child of War, but also the war-mind is favourable to violence. In old days disbanded soldiers were one of the chief sources of disorder, and no one who had an opportunity of observing it will forget the curious atmosphere of unrest which existed even in this country during the months succeeding the Armistice. I remember during the summer of 1919 meeting an agricultural labourer of the most placid appearance who informed me that he was in favour of Revolution, apparently as a general principle! And throughout that year and the next there were other and much more serious indications of a similar state of mind in many parts of the country. Some people assure us that the danger still continues. That is a grave exaggeration, and exaggerations never do any good. But it is true that there are elements in the Labour Party, and still more just outside it, which constitute a danger to the State. At present their doctrines have little influence. They are like disease microbes in a healthy body which so long as the body is healthy can do little harm. But if some fresh shock to our security were received, if we became again involved in serious foreign complications, if our political vitality were lowered, we might easily become the victims of revolutionary bacteria.

Peace, then, is not only a British interest, but pre-eminently a Conservative British interest, and one of the most urgent questions for us is : How can it be best secured ? Some advocate what used to be called a policy of splendid isolation, coupled with such an increase of our fighting forces as will intimidate any possible enemies. The difficulty of a policy of isolation is that it is impossible, a mere dream of visionaries. We did not intervene in the late war only because of our Treaty obligations, but because we believed that the triumph of Germany would have been both morally and materially fatal to us. Apart from all other considerations we could not allow Belgium to be crushed, and France invaded, without seriously imperilling our own safety. We are, in short, part of Europe whether we like it or not, and cannot be indifferent to European events. If a political murder at Serajevo ultimately plunged us into war, we cannot count on remaining unaffected by any political occurrence even in the most remote corner of the Continent.

Nor is the other part of the suggested policy more practical. Apart from the enormous political difficulty under present conditions of advocating increased expenditure on our fighting forces, such a policy would, by itself, give us no security. As we increased our forces others would do the same, especially if we proclaimed by a policy of isolation that they could expect no help from us, whatever their need; as they added to their strength we should have to add to ours, until the intolerable burden of such a competition would drive one or other of the parties to it into war as the only way of obtaining relief.

A variant of this policy is the suggestion that we should make an alliance with other powers strong enough to dominate Europe. Here again the political difficulty would be enormous. Unless very great care were taken such an alliance would merely serve to excite the enmity of the rest of the world. Counter alliances would follow, and we should find ourselves back in the state of things which preceded the World War.

What is wanted is some safeguard for our security which will not provoke the hostility of the other nations. In other words, whatever system is adopted it must be one open to all other civilised nations, for if not there will always be the danger that the countries excluded will form a nucleus of opposition. It follows, if the system of association is to be open to all, that it cannot be directed against any particular countries. Its objects must be much wider than that. Indeed, to achieve security we can aim at nothing less than the preservation of the peace of the world. And by what machinery is that object to be attained ? Are we to try for an association of nations approaching to the poet's " federation of the world," with some kind of executive imposing its decrees by organised force ? In the future, possibly. At the present time that is not a practical proposition. The nations are too far apart, too tenacious of their individual sovereignty to tolerate any plan of the kind. But short of that a great deal may be, and indeed has been, done at Geneva. The fundamental conception is that if you can only bring disputants into a room and persuade them to talk over their quarrel in a neutral atmosphere the great probability is that they will not fight. Each side will feel so anxious to preserve the sympathy of the onlooking world that they will put their case as reasonably as possible, and then either it will be found that between the contentions so reasonably stated there is really very little difference, or one of them will be found to be putting forward what really is an altogether untenable proposition, and will have to give way. The old maxim is still true, *securus judicat orbis terrarum*. What has hitherto been wanting has been the machinery by which the whole world can arrive at a judgment. That is what the League of Nations supplies. It is a forum in which the nations of the world can meet, can arrange their co-operation in matters of common interest like transit, health, humanity, etc., and can discuss openly in a calm and neutral atmosphere their subjects of dispute.

It will be seen that this is no vague project of " toshy " sentimentality. It is a carefully thought out and practical proposition in the elaboration of which some of the most practical statesmen of the world have been at work. The best tribute to its soundness is that it has succeeded. It has, in fact, procured the settlement of some half-dozen dangerous disputes. It has arranged a number of international conventions simplifying and encouraging trade and commerce. It has contributed to the prevention of disease and it has mitigated the sufferings of hundreds of thousands of human beings. That is pretty well for an institution which has been in existence just over four years.   Personally I have no doubt it will do much more, may even in time render war obsolete, but for one great danger.   There is always the chance that a strong nation, believing that it can crush its adversary rapidly, may rush into war before the machinery of the League has time to act.   This was a danger foreseen by the framers of the League, and they laid it down that no country was to resort to war until full opportunity had been given for discussion. A breach of this obligation was to entail the severest blockade by all other members of the League, followed if necessary by military action.   Even so, an arrogant and powerful nation might risk these penalties and make a sudden attack, particularly if it believed that its armaments were such as to ensure for it the victory. That is why a general and agreed reduction and limitation of armaments is so necessary for peace.   As long as nations are fully and aggressively armed there is always a risk that the rifles will go off of themselves.

There is one aspect of this international menace which ought to appeal specially to our Party.   We have, as I have said, traditionally stood for peace. But it has been peace with honour.   We have always recognised that the only secure basis for international peace must be justice.   Though rightly averse from fussy interference in the internal affairs of other nations, we have nevertheless insisted on the evils and dangers of oppression.   Above all we have set ourselves against any paltering with international obligations.   In a word, we have never been slow to

recognise the great power and consequent responsibility of the British Empire.   It must be therefore a
matter of some anxiety to us that the course of events
since the War has seriously weakened our relative
strength amongst the nations of the world.   We have
accepted a standard for our capital ships lower than
we have ever before contemplated.   We find ourselves alarmingly weak in the air compared with other
neighbouring States.   Our army has been reduced
below our pre-war figure, which was small enough
for liabilities sensibly less than those which we now
have to bear.   Nor is it practicable in our present
economic difficulties materially to increase our forces
even if that were in itself a desirable course.   Ultimately relative armed strength may become unim-
portant.   But in the present transitional stage of
international development that is not so, and the only
way to preserve our proper position among other
nations is to induce them to adopt something like
our standard of armaments.   Moreover, we are under
obligation by the Treaties of Peace to attempt to do
so.   The other nations are not in principle averse
from such a policy provided they are given some
international security from aggression more precise
than that provided by the League.   Is not this a
great opportunity for a foreign policy aiming both at
the maintenance of peace and the rehabilitation of
British authority in Europe ?   Can we not throw
ourselves into the cause of a general limitation of
armaments ?   By doing so the Tory Party would

show the country that it still stands for its peaceful traditions, would give to the young Conservatives a cause worth fighting for, and would prove once again that though other parties may talk we are the party of efficiency and action !

V

NATIONALISM AND INTERNATIONALISM
(1926)

THE Assembly of the League of Nations which met in September 1926 was in one respect memorable. It saw the admission of Germany to the League. No one who was present at the sitting when it took place will easily forget it : the hall crowded to suffocation, the dignified allocution from the Chair, the entry of the German delegates and the speeches by Herr Stresemann and M. Briand. Opinions differed as to the oratorical excellence of the two utterances. But as to the dramatic intensity of the scene there could be no question. Here was the real end of the war. At last peace was established. Europe was no longer divided into two groups. Germany had been readmitted to the comity of nations and her sponsor was France. Geneva had effaced the evil memories of Versailles.

Nor was it only the dramatic quality of the event that made it noteworthy. The admission of Germany to the League, bringing with it the ratification of the Locarno agreements, put an end, as we trust, to one of the bloodiest chapters of European history.

For centuries there has been at the best but an armed truce between France and Germany. The latent hostility of the two countries has made European peace precarious and unreal. Now there is hope of a genuine change in their relations. The League and Locarno may be the basis of a lasting Franco-German friendship.

And from the strictly League point of view the adhesion of Germany is of great value. She brings to the discussions at Geneva a new point of view and her own special national qualities of thoroughness and organisation which are of the utmost service to the League. It is of not less importance that German membership means a large addition to the League's authority and prestige and puts an end to all the rather foolish talk about its being a League of victors. In a word, the entry of Germany marks a stage in the onward march of the League towards that goal of universality which is essential for its full success.

The occasion is therefore not inopportune to review the international position. I do not mean the actual relations of the countries of Europe or the world to one another. Even if I were competent to do that it is doubtful if it would be desirable to make the attempt. But it may perhaps be more profitable to try to examine the international tendencies of the time. Now, as for many years past, we see the two forces of nationalism and internationalism apparently antagonistic or at least competing. If this competition is real and inevitable, if no accommodation is possible between them, the hope of permanent peace must be abandoned. For peace, permanent peace, depends on the triumph of internationalism as I shall presently describe it. But nationalism is so strong and in many ways so admirable a quality of mankind that if it be really the antithesis of internationalism the success of the latter becomes very improbable. Personally I believe that such an antithesis is utterly misleading, and the following observations are an effort to give my reasons for that conviction.

The League of Nations is an attempt to organise international co-operation, chiefly, no doubt, for the maintenance of peace, but also for other purposes. It is essentially an experiment in internationalism, and in this aspect is based upon the conception that a nation has more to gain from working with its fellow nations than it has from isolation. " Splendid isolation " is after all but a grand name for national selfishness, and the nation which will do nothing for its fellows can in time of need expect nothing from them. If there is any novelty in this idea it is only in its application to nations. With respect to individuals it has long been a commonplace. Indeed, civilisation is little more than the progress from isolation to co-operation. The savage man roamed the forests and jungles by himself. His first step was acceptance of family life. Then came the clan, expanding to a tribe and later a nation. Further developments followed. The nation might become part of an empire, a commonwealth of nations.   In any case it would retain its own corporate existence, and as life became more complicated it would create within itself a number of subsidiary corporate organisations for every kind of purpose.   In the modern State these organisations are very numerous. They extend over the whole range of human activity —religion, science, literature, art, recreation, fighting. And they all rest on the principle of co-operation, the principle that two men are not twice but more than twice as effective as one man, for each supplies something which the other has not got.

If this be true of men, why should it not be true of nations ?   They certainly have different character-istics, different qualities.   We may not agree what those qualities are.   But we shall be all of one mind in saying that the Briton differs from the Frenchman, that they each are distinct from the German, the Italian, the Spaniard and other Europeans, and still more from the Asiatic or the African.   Unless, then, we take the view, which perhaps some of us incline to, that the Briton is perfect and the " lesser breeds " merely lack some or all of his qualities, it seems to follow that in combination the nations will attain greater results than any one of them singly can hope to reach.   Even apart from their moral and intel-lectual attainments, the diversity of their material possessions and environment enforces the advantage of co-operation.

All this seems very obvious, and yet until lately

international relations were based on a precisely opposite theory. Each nation regarded the others as potential enemies. War was admitted to be an evil to be avoided so long as possible. But it was the *ultima ratio* of all the more important international relations. Even during peace time it could never be forgotten. Since at some time or other any two nations might be enemies in the field, they must view each other's prosperity with mixed feelings. True, the prosperity of each is the prosperity of all. Rich buyers make rich sellers. But since riches can be converted into armaments it may well be that the prosperity of another nation, though it may contribute to the present well-being of its neighbour, may ultimately prove her destruction. Hence all the economic theories of the self-contained State or Empire, high protection and cut-throat commercial competition. War, as a writer in a daily journal put it, is but intensified peace.

Nor can it be said that these theories have been abandoned even at Geneva. On the contrary, recent events have shown that they are still very much in evidence. But internationalism has made progress, meaning, as I have said, by internationalism the recognition that apart from the never-forgotten possibility of war the common interests of the nations enormously outweigh or rather absorb the individual interests of any one of them. It is on this basis that all the work of the League proceeds. If it intervenes to prevent Greece and Bulgaria resorting to war as a settlement of their differences it does so not merely to save those two countries from all the horrors we know so well, still less because it is the interest of this or that great Power that one or other of the disputants should not be crushed, but because peace is the greatest interest of each and every member of the League. If the announcement that France or Belgium or some other country has signed the so-called optional clause of the Statute of the Permanent Court of International Justice is greeted with general cheers in the Assembly, it is because the fact that an additional State has accepted the principle of compulsory arbitration in justiciable international disputes is felt to be a benefit not only to the new signatory but to the whole world. The improvement of labour conditions in the various countries, the reform of world-hygiene, the fight against the trade in noxious drugs, or the horrible traffic in women and children, even, in some of its aspects, the promotion of child welfare, though they may involve interference with what are alleged to be national interests, are none the less approved—because they serve larger and more important international objects. Indeed, in League discussions you will rarely hear objections raised to a proposal on the ground that it is not in the interest of some particular country. That consideration is naturally not forgotten. But it is usually put in a generalised form, the argument taking the shape that the suggested change would not be of international advantage. Thus when the recent questionnaire of the Mandates Commission was the subject of discussion it was not suggested that this or that question in it might embarrass a particular Mandatory, but rather that too meticulous enquiries might make it impossible for Mandatories in general to carry out their duties properly.

The instances I have given are all concerned with the direct material interests of the co-operating nations. But the same spirit has been even more obvious where no such interest is involved. I well remember in the First Assembly, when it was still doubtful whether it would ever develop a corporate unity, it was an appeal, eventually fruitless, for the nations there represented to come to the assistance of Armenia that first brought them together and made it clear that nations of the most diverse culture and characteristics could yet co-operate for a purpose materially indifferent to them all. Nor can any of those who were present when Austria besought the help of the League, which has been so triumphantly given, doubt that the immediate response of the Assembly was largely altruistic. Indeed, nations, like men, co-operate more wholeheartedly when their individual interests are not directly in question. Self-interest is mainly a centrifugal force; it is sacrifice for a common ideal that brings men and States together.

It is only to be expected that the growth of the international spirit should be, as it is, precarious. Nationalism may perhaps be defined as aggressive patriotism. Patriotism is, of course, a splendid thing. We all saw how in the War it transfigured ordinary men into heroes. It has enabled some of the greatest men in history to do some of their greatest deeds and it has inspired whole nations with the devotion and self-sacrifice of martyrs. Nevertheless, if patriotism passes into a certain type of nationalism it may become a grave evil. When Dr. Johnson said that patriotism was the last refuge of a scoundrel he was thinking of the self-styled patriots of his day who would now be called extreme nationalists. He had in mind the kind of man who says " My country, right or wrong," " Deutschland über alles," who inspires the Yellow Press and stump orators of the world to stir up enmity between peoples and ultimately to send to suffering and death tens of thousands of the best and bravest of their fellow-countrymen. Not that all nationalists are like this. There is every variety of them, from men who are little more than outspoken patriots to those who are the prey of xenophobic mania. Just because many of them are both admirable and energetic, they commonly wield great influence in their countries. We saw proof of this in the action of certain States during the controversy over the composition of the Council. The policy of the various States reflected the degrees of the nationalism of their citizens. Thus one State went so far as to vote against the award of a permanent seat in the Council to Germany, not because she doubted the propriety of that being done, but

because the other members of the Council were not
prepared to give her also a permanent seat. Here
seems a clear case of preference for national over
international interests. If such a spirit spread it
must evidently bring the League to an end. Another
State has given notice of resignation from the League
for similar reasons. According to their public
statements her Government believe that in so doing
they are quite loyal to the League. It is difficult to
agree with them. Another state, Poland, pressed
her claim to a permanent seat very strongly. But
when it became clear that this could not be granted
she decided nevertheless to continue her co-operation
with the League. Her action is a good example of
the distinction between patriotism and nationalism.
The Polish nation have given many proofs of their
patriotism. They have now shown that the most
ardent patriots may recognise that their duty to
humanity is higher even than their duty to their
country. Sweden and Czecho-Slovakia went still
further, for they were ready to resign their seats on
the Council if by that means the difficulties of the
so-called League crisis could have been resolved.

The events of March 1926, therefore, were in
some ways encouraging. I am not sure that the
manœuvres of September by which some of the
States sought for seats on the reconstituted Council
were not more disconcerting. Certainly they were
very sordid. The best that can be said for them is
that they showed how desirable Council seats have

become.   But they also showed the great strength of national feeling, even in the atmosphere of Geneva. That is a fact which must never be forgotten.   Those who framed the Covenant were fully aware of it. They knew that the League could only succeed if it avoided interference with national sovereignty and independence to the utmost extent consistently with the achievement of the great object of the League— namely, the maintenance of peace.   In two respects does this preoccupation appear in the Covenant. In the first place, the machinery of the League works normally by co-operation and not by coercion.   The one exception is that if a State rushes into war in breach of its covenant not to do so till all other means of settling the dispute have been tried, then it is to be outlawed from the comity of nations.   In all other cases, whether it be for the settlement of inter-national disputes or the furtherance of joint inter-national action, the machinery indicated is open conference—discussion and publicity ;   in other words, complete respect for national sovereignty. Secondly, even these activities of the League are confined to matters of international concern.   It is not to intervene at all in the exclusively national affairs of its members.

An examination of the Articles of the Covenant brings this out very clearly.   Thus, in the Preamble of the Covenant, it is stated to have been agreed to for the purpose of (1) promoting international co-operation and (2) achieving international peace and security. Further, international co-operation is to be promoted by: first, open diplomacy; secondly, observing international law; and, thirdly, maintaining justice and a scrupulous respect for treaties in the dealings of organised peoples with one another. All these presuppose international relations. Diplomacy is only concerned with the relations of Governments. International law only comes into play as between different Governments, or their nationals, and the last heading is specifically limited to the dealings of organised peoples with one another. When you come to the Articles of the Covenant they tell the same story. Articles 1–7 relate to organisation and do not affect the matter. Articles 8–17 inclusive consist of various provisions declared to be essential for the maintenance of peace and " the good understanding between nations "; and are emphatically international.

They deal primarily with armaments, aggression and international disputes which may be likely to lead to a breach of the peace. It is to be noted that even in a dispute likely to lead to a rupture, if the matter " is solely within the jurisdiction " of one of the parties, the Council is not to attempt to pronounce upon its merits. Articles 18–21 relate to treaties, that is to say, international engagements. Article 22, which provides for Mandates, is based solely on the international question of what should be done with the colonies taken from our enemies in the late war. Nobody will suggest that this is not a

matter of international concern.   The three next
Articles deal with League action in social and economic matters, and it will be seen that they postulate
some treaty or an international bureau.   Even apart
from this requirement, all the sub-clauses of Article
23 refer to matters which have an international
repercussion such as labour conditions, the treatment
of natives, the traffic in women and children, the
traffic in dangerous drugs, the traffic in arms, communications, transit and commerce.   In the last
sub-clause which refers to the prevention and control
of disease, the League is only to take steps " in
matters of international concern."

This question came up for rather elaborate
consideration at the last Assembly,[1] on the motion of
the British Delegation.   We felt that there was a
danger that the League might be urged to take up
questions which were essentially national and not
international.   Instances of the kind have indeed
already occurred.   The Advisory Committee on
Child Welfare had recommended that all members
of the League should be urged to provide swimming
baths for school children.   It seemed to us impossible to say that the provision of swimming baths had
any international aspect.   Other people were urging
that the League should take up the question of cruelty
to animals.   Apart from certain questions of traffic
in horses and the like, it is difficult to see how this
question, important though it is, could be regarded

[1] The Assembly of 1926.

as international. Others are anxious that we should intervene in the question of the consumption of alcohol in different countries, which would surely be stretching the sphere of international action very far. This is not a trifling matter. It had already become a favourite charge against the League that it was interfering too much in matters with which it had no concern. Such a charge is particularly dangerous because it goes to strengthen the national feelings which are already suspicious of international action.

No doubt it is difficult to draw the line between what is national and what is international. At first sight it might seem that disease was essentially a national matter. But it is obvious that infectious disease may become an international matter of great moment, and even in the case of non-infectious disease international study of it may be very important to its ultimate cure. Or again, the financial situation of a country may be thought to be chiefly or even exclusively its own concern. Yet the League rightly took up the Austrian financial situation because it is clear that the collapse of any financial unit in the international system must have an effect far beyond the borders of that unit itself. Similarly, it has dealt with financial and economic problems in Hungary, Greece and Bulgaria with great advantage. How far the League's assistance in financial matters should go must be a question to be decided in each case, but it might well be that in certain countries at any rate the advice of the League's financial experts might very properly be given, though there was no direct international interest involved. Nor did the British delegation seek to make any hard and rigid definition. But they believed that it would be of service for the matter to be fully discussed so that the general principles to be observed in League action might be elucidated quite as much with a view to insisting what was within the League's sphere as in defining what was not.

Further consideration confirms this opinion. When the League started no one knew how it would develop. It was an experiment and it was right that its growth should be unfettered in all directions. Most people thought that its only serious duty was the preservation of peace. Perhaps that is true ; but not unless we recognise that international co-operation is a chief means by which that object is to be attained. In practice by far the largest quantity of the League's work consists of its economic, social and political activities, without any direct and immediate bearing on peace and war. This has grown up partly by the transfer to the League of work that before its existence was being done in other ways, and partly by the increased necessity of joint action by the nations in consequence of the complexities of modern civilisation. Whatever may have been the origin of these non-contentious activities of the League, there they are—admirable and even fascinating—getting every year larger and larger. The time has come when they must be regulated, otherwise extravagances will appear which will warp and stifle their proper and useful development. Pruning is as necessary in human organisations as it is in horticulture and forestry.

And there is a special reason for circumspection in League matters. We are all tired of declaring that the League is not a super-state—that its members need have no fear that their sovereignty and independence will be destroyed by belonging to it. The wearisome repetition of that declaration has been requisite because otherwise we should have had arrayed against the League much of that national feeling to which allusion has already been made. Nevertheless, some voluntary modification of the full rights of a sovereign State is the inevitable result of most, if not all international engagements, the Covenant included. For instance, it is the right of any nation to exact what customs duties it pleases upon the entry into its territory of goods from another country. But if it has a commercial treaty with the Government of that country by which the latter is entitled to most-favoured nation treatment, then the right of the importing country to levy duties is limited to the amount which it levies on similar goods coming from any other country. Again, it is in international law the right of any State to go to war with another State when and where it pleases. But if the two States are members of the League their rights in this respect are limited by the Articles of the Covenant to which they have both agreed. In this instance the limitation of sovereignty will perhaps not appear irksome or oppressive, though we all remember the outburst of nationalism that followed a reminder on this point in the Corfu case five years ago.

Still, in principle public opinion in most countries recognises that some restriction of the right of war is essential if civilisation is not to perish. If that restriction is to be of any use, practical means for giving effect to it must also be adopted. The Covenant indicates two such means. Firstly, there are the sanctions provided by Article 16. In case of a resort to war by a member of the League in breach of its obligations under the Covenant it is to be first boycotted and then militarily coerced. That is to say, every member of the League has agreed that it will in certain events join with other members in using its whole economic and, if necessary, military strength to prevent the Covenant-breaking State from plunging the world into war. That is an obligation vital, as I think, for the preservation of peace, and in no way to be lightly regarded. Secondly, all members of the League are bound to secure if possible a general reduction and limitation of armaments. For this purpose preparatory measures are now in progress at Geneva and those engaged in them are realising what an intricate and difficult job it is.

What is its main difficulty ? Why, simply this—how can disarmament be made palatable to nationalism ? Even in this country that is not a very simple matter. True, we are not very sensitive about our Army, because in the first place there is no international demand for its reduction. No sane man has ever suggested that it is so large as to endanger the peace of the world. Secondly, we do not rely on our Army as our main defence against invasion. It is primarily a police force whose duty it is to garrison the Empire and keep order on the more turbulent parts of our over-seas frontiers. We have never regarded our national safety as bound up with our military strength. But with the Fleet it is different, and rightly so. Our existence depends upon our command of the sea, and every public man knows how easily aroused national feeling is about naval questions. All the more credit to us, some will say, that at Washington we agreed to make a beginning of naval disarmament. Be it so, though many foreign critics hold that all we did there was to bind on the rest of the world, still more strongly than before, Anglo-American naval domination. That is a very unfair way of putting it. But it is true that at Washington we agreed to nothing which even the most nervous of nationalists could rationally regard as hazarding our naval safety. We readily agreed to an equality of capital ships between ourselves and the United States because we considered the contingency of war between us as being so remote as to be negligible. But suppose it had been some European State instead of America, what then ? Or suppose, in the interests of general disarmament we are asked to make further naval cuts, will not national feeling insist on being satisfied that nothing shall be done which will imperil our security ?

To Continental nations their armies are what our Fleet is to us, with this addition, that they have all had comparatively recent experience of what it means when that defence against invasion has broken down. May that experience never be ours ! All the more should we try to realise how military disarmament appears to a Continental European. I was talking about disarmament the other day to a Frenchman and told him that I had found in making speeches about the League in my own country, however dead an audience was, one could always get a cheer by saying the League stood for disarmament. " Ah," said he, " that just shows the difference between the two countries ! It is when they get to disarmament that our advocates of the League feel that they are getting on to delicate ground." Perfectly natural ! And remember that, even apart from anxieties about national safety, any effective scheme of disarmament must run counter to national or at least nationalist sentiment. Consider what it means. Each nation is to agree that it will not raise its national armaments beyond a certain limit without the consent of an international authority, and it must in theory at any rate consent that its armament policy may be the subject of question or discussion at Geneva. That is the very least the acceptance of an international scheme for reduction and limitation of armaments

must mean. It is no doubt true that the gain would
be enormous. With a real scheme of this kind
accepted, international security would be immeasurably increased, taxation would be continuously
diminished, and industrial and commercial prosperity
might be expected to have such a boom as it has
never known. But those are the ultimate benefits
of the policy, and it requires for their acknowledg-
ment the rarest of all political qualities—imagination.
In the meantime, the diminution of national sovereignty, the interference of the foreigner in our own
concerns, is a topic easily available for platform and
journalistic eloquence.

It is because the League has before it such vast
and difficult duties that its influence and authority
must be preserved even, sometimes, from some of its
best friends. I am not indeed afraid of its doing too
much, provided the work is in itself worth doing and
does not affront the best kind of national feeling. So
long as any worth-while action is genuinely international, so long as it is concerned with the relations
between States, so long as it requires international
co-operation to carry it through, so long as it makes
for international knowledge and friendship—the
more work of that kind is done by the League, the
better for it and for the world. The fact that any
particular proposal is resented in one country or
another need not necessarily involve its rejection,
though, of course, the opinions and even prejudices
of every country must be given due consideration.

The constitution of the League and the rule of unanimity preclude anything like rash international action. But interference or threat of interference with exclusively national concerns cannot be defended, and if indulged in will greatly increase the sensitiveness of national feeling towards proposals, such as disarmament, vital to international life, which yet involve some infringement of the theoretic perfection of national sovereignty. It is therefore of great importance that in respect to national susceptibilities the League should walk cautiously. But a negative policy of that kind is altogether inadequate. National feeling towards the League should not be merely acquiescent, it should be one of its chief supports. There is no reason why it should not be so. Loyalty to a smaller organisation need not be any hindrance to loyalty to the larger organisation in which it is included. A county cricketer if he is a sportsman will not become less keen for his county's success because he is also a member of the England Eleven against Australia. A soldier's *esprit de corps* applies not less to the British Army than it does to his regiment. In times past it was thought to be an object of statesmanship to produce uniformity of language and thought, of religion and ideals among all the subjects of the Empire. They were all to be made not only good Britons but as far as possible good Englishmen. Luckily, after some disastrous experiments, that theory has been abandoned. More and more we foster local patriotism.   Even in this comparatively small island we recognise three nationalities, and throughout the Empire there are growing up new and autonomous nations bound together not by coercive laws but by free affection.   We have found, in short, the secret of unity in diversity.

Why should not the process which has served us so well in our Empire be applied with equal success to the world at large ?   Why should not the representatives of the nations at Geneva come to feel that the best proof of their attachment to their country is to increase their country's international influence and importance by loyal service to the League ?   I remember during the peace conference at Paris a striking incident in the Commission formed to draw up the Covenant.   The room in which we sat was not very large and was exceedingly hot and crowded. Representatives of a dozen or more nationalities were there.   President Wilson was in the chair, and in the course of the debates some question cropped up which raised the issue between nationalism and internationalism.   After the discussion had proceeded for some time the President brought it to an end by a wonderful speech in which he looked forward to the time when men would be as ashamed of being disloyal to humanity as they were now of being disloyal to their country.   His eloquence moved us all.   But many there thought him a mere visionary whose aspirations would never be fulfilled.   It may be so.   And yet sometimes, sitting in the Assembly with all its imperfections and incompleteness, I wonder if his prophecy is not coming true. Year by year the member States take it more seriously, the representatives are more influential, they are more anxious to secure its good-will. One State, which at first was content to be represented there by an unpopular professor, now regularly sends its foreign minister ; and whereas the same State used almost openly to flout the League and all its organs, it has this year been prominent among those who desired a seat in the Council. So, too, the League policy of other States has completely changed. One of them, which used to be the leader of those who wished to diminish the activity of the League and keep it in its proper place, now is anxious to convince the world that it is its chief friend, and some of its nationals even suggest that other proved friends of the League are really half-hearted—a suggestion which I regret to say has been swallowed by certain gullible individuals in this country. That may not be exactly the spirit which President Wilson had in mind—but it does show a recognition that leadership of the League has become an object of national ambition. That is a step in the right direction, surely considerable in view of the youth and immaturity of the institution. If after six years Foreign Offices are beginning to vie with one another for positions of influence in the League, what may not happen when another generation has grown up and the undergraduates of to-day are the Foreign

Ministers of to-morrow? Are we really mere visionaries if we look forward to a time when the reputation of nations will depend as much on achievements for peace as in the past it did on pre-eminence in war? I see no incredibility in such a vision. Certainly it is not patriotism or even reasonable nationalism that should stand in the way. The happiness and prosperity of mankind is no less natural an object of national ambition than skill and courage in the defeat of armies or the destruction of fleets. All depends on public opinion. If we—the people of this country and of other countries—desire that the glories of peace should take the place of the glories of war, that great and beneficent change will assuredly come to pass. And in bringing it about, may we not trust that the British nations will take no laggard or unworthy part?

VI

CO-OPERATION, THE BASIS OF PEACE
(1927)

THE two lines of criticism of the League of Nations which are probably the most effective in this country are, firstly, that it was a new-fangled fancy of President Wilson, and, secondly, that it has often been tried before and has always failed. Neither is in accordance with the facts of history, but of the two the former is the more untrue. That there are novel features about the League no one would deny. But its central idea, Co-operation as a means of progress, is as old as civilisation itself.

When Co-operation began is indeed not known, but it must have been very early in human history. It is usual to distinguish the ages of prehistoric man by his increasing mastery of tools and weapons. We speak of the Stone Age and of the Bronze Age and of the Iron Age, making the substance of the instruments used by man the criterion of his progress. But if we knew the whole truth, it is probable that the growth of co-operation was a more important factor in his history than his use of stone or metals. When we come to historical times, at any rate, his social and political advancement depends almost entirely upon the growth of co-operation. How far co-operation was an instinctive element in the hunting and fighting of prehistoric man is unknown. But apart from these occupations it is legitimate to imagine that the first step out of complete barbarism was made by the organisation of the family, and the substitution of some more or less permanent form of marriage for promiscuity. From the family doubtless developed the clan, the clan grew into the tribe, and by the coalescence of tribes the nation was brought into existence.

With the development of each larger unit went the development of the appropriate political and social organisation. The father of the family became the chief of the clan or tribe ; and with increasing power and responsibility there followed first the king, and then whatever constitution of the nation was suitable to its idiosyncrasies.

Coincident with the growth of political ideas came the elaboration of social and economic institutions, and fighting became rarer. In purely barbarous tribes combat is endemic. The savage walks through the forest with his club or tomahawk, as ready to slaughter his fellow-men as he is to kill any other animals. When he is organised in clans and tribes he no longer fights his fellow-clansmen or tribesmen, but still one of his chief occupations consists of raids and forays on other clans and tribes.

Fighting is not an elevating occupation, nor are men commonly the better for indulging in the slaughter of their fellows. It is, therefore, not surprising that as soon as the nations developed and co-operation for civil purposes increased, war was more and more recognised as an evil. In the Hebrew Prophets, for instance, the horror of it steadily increases, and even the passages in the Psalms and elsewhere, which seem to glorify fighting, regard it expressly as an instrument of God's vengeance on the people who dispute His authority and delight in war.

A similar strain, I believe, runs through all early literature. Nothing is more poignant, for instance, than the description of the horror and misery brought by war upon the Trojan women.

> "Voices of Death and mists are over them,
> Of dead men's anguish, like a diadem,
> These weak abhorr'd things that serve the hate
> Of Kings and peoples."

This attitude to war in general is quite consistent with admiration for individual deeds of courage and skill. For, in the first place, if war is to exist, victory is always preferable to defeat, so that those who contribute most to success on the field of battle will rightly reap their reward of admiration and gratitude from their fellow-countrymen. And in the second place, willingness to face death at the call of duty must always be the most glorious proof that man's nature is in some degree divine.

Broadly, then, hatred of war grows with civilisation. This is due not only to increased education, though it is obvious that the more educated a nation is, the more its people will condemn so senseless a method of settling disputes as brute force. But apart from that, the actual evil of war increases in direct proportion to the extent to which a State is civilised, for war is in truth and in fact a relic of barbarism, and the nearer a State is to barbarism the less it suffers from war.

The men of an Arab tribe ride on a *ghazzi* against their neighbours. They steal their flocks and herds and ravage the crops, with the usual accompaniment of outrage and murder. The evil is indeed very great, but it is temporary, and in the main confined to individuals who actually suffer loss or injury. The tribal life is not affected unless the slaughter or enslavement is carried very far. When the raid is over, the raided tribe, weakened and impoverished, moves a little further away and begins again its precarious existence, making plans for a counter-raid to recover its lost sheep and cattle.

But as the organisation of the tribe becomes complete, as it grows into a nation, the evil of warlike operations becomes steadily greater. The pursuits of civilised man—art, science, commerce, industry, finance—can only be carried on in time of peace. True, religion and philosophy may sometimes flourish in spite of bloodshed and disorder. But the cases where they do so are rare. Even these supreme occupations of men's highest faculties are apt to be overwhelmed by violence, or, if they survive, do so as a protest against, and a mental refuge from, a state of things to which they are by their very nature opposed.

And so we see at the present day those nations which have reached the highest degree of civil organisation are precisely those which are the most hurt by war.

There is a story of a traveller who visited one of the Balkan States and was struck by the backwardness of its institutions. He ventured to say something derogatory about the roads, railways, education, etc., to a native of the country, and was met with the reply : " True, we cannot do any of these things, but we can fight, and fight well, so we mean always to be at war." That is no doubt a libel. But it is true that the less complex the organisation of a State, the less serious will be the dislocation caused by war. And the converse is equally true, as we know to our cost.

It is now nine years since the Armistice, and in our social and economic life the scars of war are all too evident. Our moral and religious losses may be disputed ; no doubt we have gained something in apparent sincerity to compensate for the loss in self-control and the growth of materialism. Personally, I believe the balance is heavily against us even in this respect, and as to our economic losses, there is no question that our trade is only just recovering, our credit is still far from what it was in pre-war times, our taxation is intolerably heavy, and the number of our unemployed is a crying evil. There is nothing surprising in these results ; indeed, on the whole, we got off lightly. We were victorious. That saved our political institutions. Most of the countries that suffered defeat suffered also revolution. What revolution would have meant to all the elaborate financial machinery on which our prosperity depends, needs no comment from me.

Then during the war our people did not suffer economically. Employment was good, wages were high, even allowing for the increased cost of living. Above all, our food supply was not seriously restricted. It is not, perhaps, sufficiently recognised how favoured we were in that respect. The so-called Blockade was not only one of the principal factors in our victory, but it saved us from attacks on our communications which must have inflicted terrible hardships on our people, and might have brought us to defeat. That was due both to the skill and devotion of our sailors, and to the exceptional geographical conditions in which we fought. By blocking the channels of the North Sea we were able to prevent our enemies from sending out more than a few occasional raiders against our commerce. Yet even so, as Lord Jellicoe told us at Geneva, the damage they did was very severe. It is worth quoting his actual words : " In spite of the fact that when war broke out Germany had only two armoured cruisers, six light cruisers, and four armed auxiliaries outside the North Sea, our losses in merchant ships due to the action of these German vessels exceeded 220,000 tons, and the allied losses 30,000 tons, before they finally were disposed of. It must be remembered, too, that of the above force, Von Spee's Squadron of two armoured cruisers and three light cruisers was in the Pacific when war broke out, and was therefore not favourably placed for operating against trade, nor, indeed, did it attempt to do so. The existence of this powerful squadron at large had, however, a great effect upon our cruiser dispositions up to the time of the battle of the Falkland Islands. The great majority of our early losses were due to the operations of the *Emden*, the *Karlsruhe*, and three armed auxiliaries. Later in the war, three disguised German raiders accounted for 254,000 tons of British and 39,000 tons of allied shipping." Had the raiders been multiplied by ten, as they easily might be under different conditions, we should have been almost certainly defeated, by the cutting off of our supplies, even if our Naval superiority were much greater than it was in the last war.

Again, we were very lucky that air warfare was only in its embryo stage. The effect of the raids on London shook the nerve of some sections of the population and kept at home many aeroplanes that were sorely needed in France. Had aircraft existed in the hands of our enemies in numbers such as other countries now have, the results would have been very different. As General Groves observes : " The air raids of the past are no guide as to the nature of future aerial attack, or even of those which could be delivered to-day. For example, the British Air Minister stated last year that—' Whereas in the late war some 300 tons of bombs were dropped in this country by the Germans, air forces to-day could drop almost the same weight in the first twenty-four hours of war, and continue this scale of attack indefinitely.' "

In view of these considerations it may well be thought that, had things gone only a little differently in the late war, we should have suffered disaster and defeat with the almost certain accompaniment of revolution. Our margin of safety was certainly not very great. And if we had been defeated, if we had suffered so much that our political stability had been destroyed, the consequences would have been tremendous. For such an event could scarcely have failed to put an end to the British Empire.

We have quite rightly conceded something almost indistinguishable from independence to our self-governing Dominions. But it must never be forgotten that their association with one another in a commonwealth depends on the relations of each one of them with Great Britain. Take away Great Britain and the connecting link between the Dominions is destroyed. Most of all is it true that the good government of India depends entirely upon the healthy condition of British Sovereignty.

The conclusions, then, that we have so far reached are that co-operation between individuals is essential to the first steps of civilisation, and that the higher the civilisation, the greater the co-operation. Further, we have seen that war—fighting—which is definitely the antithesis to international co-operation and destroys it, is also the greatest enemy of civilised progress. Where you have a state of society in which civilisation is not very far advanced, and is consequently not very complex, that is to say, where co-operation between the individuals or the bodies composing the State is confined to the simplest relations of man, there the dislocation caused by fighting is not very great. But where you have a political organisation such as the British Empire, which is exceedingly elaborate and complex, and a number of social and political arrangements, such as we have in this country, which are the result of years of growth and depend on institutions elaborately constructed to meet the special circumstances of this country—in such a case as that the consequence of war will be proportionately disastrous. That is true inside Great Britain and the British Commonwealth. It is also true of our relations to foreign countries.

The state of things in which each nation can live on its own resources, having very little to do with other nations, belongs to an age which has quite passed, at any rate in Western Europe. International jurists, who used to be so much concerned

with the independence of States, are turning attention more and more to their interdependence.
Politically, commercially, intellectually, in every
branch of human activity, the nations become less
and less self-supporting. As Lord Birkenhead said
at Frankfort the other day, " Europe is, after all,
interdependent. The prosperity of one constituent
nation will be increased, not diminished, by the
prosperity of another."

Every year sees improvements in European inter-
communications, so that it will soon be easy to reach
almost any part of Europe from London in less than
twenty-four hours. Even now, men can talk to one
another across whole continents, and listeners-in in
the remotest parts of Central and Eastern Europe
can hear the lectures and concerts of Savoy Hill. I
read somewhere that when Pascal was carrying out
some of his barometrical experiments, the details
only became known two or three years later in Rome.
Till little more than a century ago there was no such
thing as a daily newspaper ; and important news
still had to be carried by hand until the middle of
last century.

It is therefore quite natural and right that those
who drew up the Covenant in 1919 should have
placed in the forefront of the objects for which the
League of Nations exists that of promoting international co-operation. That is the true road of
international progress, and the League, which is
the latest effort in that direction, rightly enshrines

this principle in the first words of its fundamental statute.

There are, in fact, two broad aspects of the Covenant, of which the first is the building up of co-operation between nations. That has been going on for a long time. In Mr. Leonard Woolf's *International Government* is given a description of the great number of international activities which existed before the League came into existence. Things like the Postal Union, the various health conventions, the fight against opium and noxious drugs, and other social evils ; the traffic on certain international rivers ; and a number of other arrangements, commercial, social, scientific, and so on, were regulated by special agreements between nations. What the League did in this respect was to hasten the process and to concentrate it more and more in one centre— Geneva. For the first time in the world's history we have an international organisation always in existence and always working at the various problems of international co-operation.

The case of Opium will illustrate my meaning. The Hague Convention on Opium was drafted at the Hague Conference in 1912. But it was not till the Paris Conference in 1919, at which the Covenant was agreed to, that it was accepted by any considerable number of States. Since that time the Opium Commission has been created by the League. It meets periodically at Geneva and studies the development of the Opium problem, making from time to time recommendations for further action. These culminated in the Opium Conference of 1924-5, at which two further conventions were agreed to, and the machinery of the League is now being employed to secure the ratification of these conventions. Here, then, the League has been utilised, first as a means of bringing nations into consultation ; secondly, as an instrument for drafting the necessary conventions to cope with the evils so brought to light ; and thirdly, as a lever to press the governments to ratify them. When this has been done, there will be a fourth activity to be discharged by the League, namely, to see that the conventions are carried out.

I have given this instance of the work of the League in fostering international co-operation on the old lines, and I might give many more such instances, extending over almost every branch of social, political, and commercial activity. And besides this, the League has been instrumental in setting on foot new forms of international co-operation. The financial rescue of Austria is an instance of the kind of thing I mean. There the leading financial powers of the world combined together to give financial assistance to Austria on the terms that she would accept League advice and direction in her financial rehabilitation. The result has been extremely successful. Austria is now financially on her feet, and unless she does something foolish there is no reason why she should not steadily advance to prosperity. A similar work was undertaken for

Hungary, and one is in contemplation for Bulgaria. Greece was aided in rather a different form in order to enable her to cope with the great financial strain caused by the enormous influx of refugees at the close of the Turkish war. Other countries have asked for or accepted financial advice from the League. In all these cases the actual and direct result of the international co-operation has been beneficial to the countries concerned, and has advanced various social or philanthropic causes. Indirectly, something has been done to bring the nations closer together, and to make them realise their interdependence. But the results are necessarily precarious so long as the danger of war exists, for war would sweep away in a few weeks all the success that has been attained.

It is therefore in order to make international co-operation in peace possible that the League uses it in trying directly to abolish war. Thus a series of provisions in the Covenant exists with the object of preventing the outbreak of war, or limiting its consequences. By Article 11, every member of the League is given the right to bring to the notice of the Council or the Assembly any circumstances likely to disturb international relations, and the League is directed to take what action it thinks right in the circumstances. This is the strictly preventive function of the League, giving it the right to interfere before dangerous disputes have actually taken place. On the whole, this Article is the one which has been of the greatest value in the League history. In several instances it has been put into force, and the action taken by the League under it has been of great value.

Next follow a group of Articles designed to deal with disputes when they have actually arisen. The purpose of the Articles is to facilitate the reference of any such disputes as are capable of judicial or arbitral decision to the Permanent Court of International Justice or to arbitration, while all other disputes, if they are of a character likely to lead to a rupture of diplomatic relations, are to be dealt with by the Council of the League in its consultative capacity. Here, however, an obvious difficulty arises. The Council can only decide unanimously. What happens if the Council is not unanimous, excluding, of course, the parties to the dispute ? In that case, under the Covenant, nothing happens, and the dispute is left to take its course. This is what is referred to in League discussions as " the Gap," and there are many reformers who are anxious to see some provision by which this gap can be closed. It is true that in practice the importance of the gap might not be very great. If a dispute were referred to the Council, and the majority of that body expressed their opinion in favour of one or other of the disputants, it is most unlikely that the other disputant would carry the matter further. But the moral effect of the existence of the gap is considerable. In the atmosphere of nervousness and suspicion which unhappily exists in so many continental countries, the existence of the gap is constantly referred to as proving that the security afforded by the Covenant is not a real thing. And there can be no doubt that it would be desirable from this point of view to close the gap, if that could be done without causing other and worse difficulties.

Another reform should, in my judgment, be carried out, as and when it is possible. The Council of the League is not a judicial body, and its dealing with disputes in which important countries are involved is coloured very much by the political feelings of the members of the Council. There is a tendency for them to utilise arguments more of expediency than of equity, and methods more parliamentary than jurisprudential, which does not conduce to the triumph of justice or to the appeasement of angry and suspicious feelings. The more, therefore, that international disputes can be transferred from the political atmosphere of the Council to the judicial atmosphere of the Permanent Court, the better will be the results, both actual and moral.

One other observation on this part of the Covenant machinery is worth making. The sanction provided by the Covenant is that contained in Article 16. To the penalties of that Article any State which has broken its obligations under the dispute clauses of the Covenant is amenable. But the application of the Article does not depend on any decision of the

Council. It is for each of the members of the League to judge when the *casus fœderis* has arisen. It has, indeed, been proposed by the Assembly that the Council should express an opinion on the subject. But even so, that opinion would not be binding on any member of the League, though it might be a guide to its action.

With regard to international disputes, then, the scheme of the Covenant is that all disputes shall be submitted to arbitration or judicial decision or to the opinion of the Council ; that if they are submitted to arbitration or judicial decision, then the parties are bound by the result ; but if they go to the consideration of the Council, and the Council is not unanimous, no one, in form at any rate, is bound. If any State resorts to war in breach of these obligations, then the provisions of Article 16 apply, which involve severance of all relations between the offending country and other Members of the League in the first place, and military action, if necessary, later on. But the question of whether any State has broken its obligations is left to be determined by each of the other members of the League after considering all the circumstances of the case, including any opinion which the Council may have given on the subject.

It must be admitted that this scheme is far from perfect, and it is not surprising that League reformers have desired to complete it and make it more definite. Still, if it can be relied upon, it is probably sufficient to have prevented any of the wars of recent history from having taken place.

A much more formidable objection to it is the doubt whether in point of fact these provisions would ever be put into force. That is a doubt which the future alone can resolve. It is, for instance, commonly said that it would be very difficult to induce the nations to put in force Article 16 if the " resort to war " took place in order to right some international wrong. Suppose that under the existing treaties it turns out that some territorial arrangement is contrary to the wishes of the inhabitants and to the justice of the case, and the nation, aggrieved by this state of things, tries to set it right forcibly. Would the other members of the League intervene to perpetuate what they believe to be an unjust settlement ? I do not myself feel this argument very strongly, for two reasons. In the first place, the object is to prevent breaches of the peace. And they may be just as disastrous to the well-being of Europe or the world whether the cause of the quarrel is just or unjust. We in England have recognised for a very long time that a man must not take the law into his own hands. Ever since the days of Richard II, at any rate, it has been a criminal offence to expel a man by violence from property which he has wrongly occupied, and I am prepared myself to defend a similar provision in international law. Secondly, there is no justification now for redress of injustice by violence, for another remedy is provided in the

Covenant. By Article 19 the Assembly is given power to revise treaties which are no longer in accordance with what is right and fair. True, the Assembly can only act with unanimity, but the moral effect of decision by an overwhelming majority that a particular state of things was not right or fair would make it almost impossible nowadays for such a condition to be maintained.

There is, however, one thing that may be said with great certainty. As long as the nations are building up great competitive armaments there is no probability that this or any other machinery for peace will be effective. That is why the Reduction and Limitation of Armaments is so vital to the success of the League of Nations. I do not say that without that reduction and limitation the League is useless ; but I do say that its principal duty, the duty of maintaining the peace of the world, becomes enormously more difficult, and may indeed be almost impossible.

All nations admit this more or less. No voice has ever been found at the Assembly to defend the great armaments that still exist in the world, still less their probable development if nothing is done to check them. Nevertheless they persist, and in some respects continue to grow. The air forces of the different countries, for instance, are constantly, and in some cases rapidly, increasing, and there can be no question that in each country the increase is due to the fear of what the other countries are doing. Even taking armaments as a whole, the comparison with 1913 is not altogether reassuring. Take the test of expenditure. Some countries are spending much less. France, allowing for present values, has cut down her expenditure by nearly 50 per cent. Italy is down 40 per cent. Germany, under the operation of the Versailles Treaty, is spending 65 per cent. less than she was. But we are spending at least as much. Indeed, in the calculations that I have seen we are spending a little more than we were in 1913. And the United States of America seems to be spending 25 per cent. more than she was before the war. It is no doubt true that these figures do not necessarily correspond with the armed strength of the nations. But they do not indicate any drastic reduction, except in Germany. Competition in armaments has paused, but it has not ceased, and so long as it continues it is inconsistent with international co-operation. So far as armaments are competitive they depend on the danger of war. They may be said to threaten war. I lay stress on the word competitive because that is the test of whether armaments are a danger to peace or not. It can well be conceived that countries will always have to maintain certain armaments, if for no other purpose in order that they might carry out, as Article 8 puts it, their international obligations. But the moment the size of the armaments of one country is made to depend on the size of the armaments of another, the danger arises. One has only to con-

sider what would happen in this island if England
and Scotland maintained national armies of which
the strength was regulated by regard to the armaments of each other. Evidently, the unity of
Great Britain would be at an end, and co-operation
between the two countries would become very
difficult. In the case of Great Britain a joint army
is maintained, and so far from becoming a danger
to the unity of the country, it is a sign and seal of
such unity.

That a common army can be maintained by the
States of Europe is not at present within the range
of practical politics. But it is conceivable that the
armies of all the States should be maintained for one
common purpose, namely, preservation of peace ;
and many of us believe that it is upon that footing
that the armies not only of Europe but of England
and America ought to be considered. Had that
view been the governing view during the recent
negotiations at Geneva, agreement would have been
not only possible but easy.

What, then, of the future ? If we are to listen to
the teaching of history we must perceive that the
line of progress is the line of international co-operation. That must be fostered by all means in our
power. As a first step we must get rid of the idea
of competitive armaments, and for that purpose
reduce and, still more, limit the armaments that
exist. That seems to be a step without which there
is no hope of progress. And it can be facilitated

and completed by a general substitution of law for war as the means for settling international disputes. All the different ways of arbitration, therefore, are to be advocated. Above all, we must get rid of the misconception that war is natural or inevitable. It is, in fact, quite unnatural and ought to be easily avoided. After all, at the present time the most common cause of war is international fear and suspicion. Can anything be more absurd or unreasonable than that nations should fight one another because they are afraid of doing so ? Lay aside fear and the necessity for fighting would be gone.

No doubt there are other causes of war. There are the strong ties of nationality stretching over artificial and ill-settled boundaries. These depend very largely on the conception that nations are all potential enemies of one another. Get rid of that idea and the bitterness of boundary disputes disappears. No one thinks of getting into a state of any real agitation about the national boundaries in this country. When I was young, the county of Monmouth was part of England, or was said to be in the geography books. Now it is considered part of Wales, and I never heard that that seriously hurt the feelings of any Englishman or caused undue rejoicing in the breast of a Welshman !

There is no reason in the nature of things why boundaries between European countries should be more important. Napoleon declared that war was an anachronism, and that whoever troubled the peace of Europe wanted civil war. That is true. In modern times and under modern conditions the nations of Europe belong to one social and political unity. Their common interests are far greater and far more important than their rivalries. I have already quoted Lord Birkenhead's recent observations on the interdependence of the European nations. And I most heartily agree with him. True, we are a very long way from any formal federation of Europe, but there seems no reason why we should not reach at no very distant period a state of international feeling which would make most of the disputes that now agitate the European community futile and unreal.

To reach that result all that seems necessary is to press forward international co-operation and to sweep from its path those competitive armaments which are its principal obstacle and its chief danger.

But can this be done? And if so, how? Much has been said about the difficulty of the Reduction and Limitation of Armaments, and no doubt the technical difficulties are great. If you fix your mind solely on such difficulties, they will very soon grow to be insuperable. But they are not insuperable, in fact; far from it. Everyone knows that any nation can, if it likes, reduce and limit its own armaments. We have done so, both in the Army and Navy, since the war. And other countries have done the like. If, then, each country can reduce and limit its armaments, it is evident that all of them can agree to do it together. The real point is, will they do it? And that entirely depends on whether they think it safe to do so. So that it comes round always, sooner or later, to the question of Security. That is what they found once again, this year [1] at Geneva, and the Assembly of the League laid down certain very valuable principles which, if acted upon, would undoubtedly produce reduction and limitation of armaments.

Security is partly psychological and partly material. If all the nations believed they were safe, they would be safe. If you take away from them all means of causing danger to their neighbours, that also would produce security.

To achieve security, then, two roads are open to us. One is to turn the thoughts of the nations away from war; and that can be done by promoting the peaceful settlement of international disputes, particularly by arbitration, taken in its widest sense. But no amount of agreements for arbitration will reassure anxious nations if they see their neighbours are armed to the teeth. That is why, even psychologically, the reduction and limitation of armaments is of vital importance.

There is another way in which you can create material security, that is by convincing the nations that they will not have to rely solely on their own resources in case they are the victim of an aggression. That is pointed out with great clearness in the

[1] 1927.

Resolution of the late Assembly at Geneva. For this purpose the Assembly advocated the systematic preparation of action under Article 11, which, as I reminded you earlier, is the Article which aims at the prevention of war rather than its cure after it has broken out, which is the function of Article 16.

The terms of Article 11 are very wide, and very vague, and it is urged that increased precision might be given to the Article without extending its meaning. For instance, one might point out the various measures short of actual coercion which might be used to avert a threatening international situation. You might begin by the withdrawal of the diplomatic representatives of all the nations belonging to the League from the capital of either or both of the States in dispute. That would be a most impressive demonstration. If that failed, something in the nature of a naval, or even an aerial, demonstration might be tried, again on behalf of all the members of the League. I cannot believe myself that if steps of this kind were taken any nation would be so reckless as to persist in action which might bring upon it the active hostility as well as the moral disapproval of almost the whole civilised world.

It is, no doubt, difficult to prepare machinery of actual coercion under Article 16 until the occasion arises, because the circumstances in which such coercion may be called for are so infinitely various. But it was suggested by the Finnish delegation, and the British Government gave its support to the suggestion, that measures should be taken beforehand by which financial support might be available for a country which was the victim of an aggression. Financial machinery might be prepared on the lines of the international assistance to Austria, so that any such country would be certain of being given means of preparing its own defence. This would have two advantages. It would greatly increase the sense of reality of the measures possible under Article 16. And it would diminish the necessity for expensive reserve preparation before war broke out.

Finally, there is the celebrated Gap of which I have already spoken, and on that point every consideration might be given as to what we can do to close it.

Once you get the feeling of security amongst the nations in Europe, there is no doubt that the deliberations of such a body as the Preparatory Commission become infinitely more actual. I was very much struck last spring by the underlying feeling of so many of the Continental nations that it was not much use making preparations for a Conference on Disarmament unless the nations who took part in it really meant business ; and they will not mean business unless they feel reduction and limitation of armaments have become practical politics.

Certainly now is the time if we are going to do anything. We must act before the recollection of the late war has faded from our memories. That was the great incentive to action in 1920. That was what made the acceptance of the Covenant of the League of Nations a possibility. And that recollection is still with us. Moreover, as has recently been pointed out, Europe is very far from having settled down. Threats of war are still flying about the more disturbed parts of the Continent. Many nations are profoundly dissatisfied with existing conditions, and in some of them men are found who say that a fresh appeal to arms is the only way to end their injustice. But though those feelings exist to remind us that the danger of war is by no means at an end, yet on the whole the overwhelming feeling of the population of the world is in favour of peace and reduction of armaments.

I am profoundly convinced that that is so, and that the efforts and suggestions made in successive Assemblies of the League of Nations by all those assembled there are not mere rhetorical flourishes, but are the expression of the deep desires of the nations which they represent.

And in this movement what should be our attitude ? Surely not one of indifference ; still less of reprobation. Our interests, our history, the genius of our people, all combine to make it essential that we should lead the forces of peace and disarmamen, and not discourage them. And our opportunity for doing so is great. No one doubts that we have to a very marked degree the confidence of other nations. They may be disappointed in our actions, they may criticise our attitude, but they do trust us ;

partly, let us hope, for our merits ; partly because in a way we stand aloof from the great Continental controversies. There is scarcely a great nation in Europe that does not earnestly desire our friendship. France, Germany, Italy, all alike are anxious to stand well in our good graces. Nor am I sure, in spite of many superficial ebullitions to the contrary, that the same may not be said even of Soviet Russia.

We had a great example of what we can do at Locarno. No doubt the first idea of Locarno came from the Germans, and without the support of France it could evidently have gone no further. But all the same, nothing could have been done without us. If we had not been prepared to guarantee the Franco-German frontier, the two countries primarily concerned would never have made the agreement at which they arrived in 1925.

I certainly am not an advocate for extending the obligations we undertook at Locarno to other parts of Europe. They are far too onerous. If I cite the example of Locarno, it is not necessarily as one that ought to be imitated elsewhere, but rather as showing the enormous influence we do possess in Europe. It is not too much to say that, if we oppose any international proposal, it is bound to fail ; and if we support it, it is almost certain that it can be made successful. For the moment, for the next few years, how long no one can say, the future of Europe is in our hands more than in those of any other nation. Our opportunity is great ; our responsibility is proportionate. I believe we can save Europe from future war if we have courage and vision, and I am certain that if we have not that courage and that vision the future of Europe is black indeed.

VII

THE MORAL BASIS OF THE LEAGUE OF NATIONS

(1923)

IT may seem scarcely necessary to prove a truth so obvious as that the League of Nations must have a moral basis. The League of Nations stands for peace as opposed to war, for co-operation between the nations as opposed to hostility ; and it does not seem possible for anyone, however prejudiced he may be, to doubt that there is a moral basis for such a movement as that. And yet the conclusion is not quite so clear as it appears to be on the surface. Certain it is—and we must recognise it as a fact— that there are good men and women who are opposed to the League of Nations. There are probably many more who regard it with indifference, or as a political experiment of no great importance or promise, and as to which, at any rate, they desire to reserve their judgment.

There are a certain number of such people in this country, and there are more of them in other countries. There is another land very closely allied to us in speech and in methods of thought—the United

States of America. In that country a great many people are either doubtful about the League or hostile to it. This is a fact, and these people are neither criminals nor lunatics ; on the contrary, many of them are excellent men and women. It is extremely important that we should understand the causes which have created such an attitude and the reasons which are advanced in its defence.

Some current opinions adverse to the League spring from an assumption that the maxims of morality, and especially the maxims of Christian morality, do not apply to the relations between States, as they apply to the relations between individuals. The argument, when it is openly stated and defended, is usually of this kind : " Individuals are morally bound to be unselfish, not to press their claims unduly, and to be ready to sacrifice themselves if necessary for others. But when we think of the State "—this is the argument—" we must not be misled by the phrase. We must not think of the State as if it were an individual. We must remember how in fact it is directed. Every State is governed and guided by a small number of men ; sometimes, of course, by an Absolute Sovereign, but more frequently by a Committee of Ministers, or other body of men, whose business it is to look after the interests of the great mass of the people over whom they rule. It is all very well to talk about Christian duties, or even moral duties," the critic argues, " but these Ministers have no right to be generous at the expense of the people they govern. If they are, they are not carrying out the principles of morality, for morality commands them, in the first place, to be faithful to their trust ; and their trust is to do the best they can for the people they have been selected to guide."

This is one version of an assumption which is frequently held. It is not the only version ; there are others of a more metaphysical nature, which I do not propose to consider on this occasion.

There are two answers. In the first place it may be said, and said, I think, with great truth, that in the end it is better, in the interests of the people, that their rulers should act according to the principles of morality applied to the nation as if it were an individual. What I mean is this. If a nation acquires a reputation for being untrustworthy, treacherous, or cruel, or for being guilty of other great lapses in morality, it will not be successful in the end, for the masses of the people will discover that a reputation of that kind is hostile to their interests. They will discover that it is better, even on strictly selfish grounds, to sacrifice some immediate advantage in order to observe the broad rules of morality, of justice and even of generosity, in dealing with other nations. And therefore a statesman who accepts to the full the position—which, of course, he must accept—that he is a trustee for the welfare of his fellow-countrymen, will yet do well to guide their policy in accordance with the rules of morality, because, in the end, however it may appear for the moment, it will be of the greatest advantage to the people concerned.

This is one answer, and I believe it to be a true answer. But for reasons which I shall give directly, I do not accept it as the most fundamentally true answer.

The other answer is this. I am prepared to say that the State is an individual, a moral individual, and is subject as such to the moral law. I believe that through the development of a mysterious but essential capacity of our nature, human beings can join together and make themselves, for one reason or another, into a corporate whole ; and having done so, they assume a new character, ceasing to be wholly and solely an aggregation of units, and becoming a new entity, subject to its own moral laws and moral duties.

I prefer this answer, though it may appear somewhat abstract, because I believe it to be more in accordance with reality. As a matter of fact, we all feel that we desire our country to act up to the highest standard, not so much because it will be most profitable to us in the long run, but because we want to feel that we are part of an honourable, upright, chivalrous, generous Nation. I believe that this is a very deep and pervasive feeling, which no amount of reasoning can shake. No one likes to hear his country spoken of as having done a treacherous thing or taken a mean advantage. Looking at it then from this point of view, a statesman who believes himself to be a trustee must realise the feeling which pervades the population of every country. It is, that they desire their policies to be conducted not only for their immediate advantage, but in such a way as to preserve the national honour and the national reputation.

There are many reasons in favour of this answer to the argument that the State has no moral responsibility. Among other reasons, it provides a much easier and safer guide to practical policy. A form of statecraft may be defended on the strictly utilitarian ground of what will be for the greatest immediate advantage of the State, and this consideration theoretically may perhaps produce the same results, if carried out with great wisdom and great circumspection, as the simpler method of trying to do the right and generous and honourable thing : but it is much more likely to lead the nation into error and disaster.

We have seen this in modern times in the influence of the school of which Treitschke and Bernhardi are the best known exponents. Their conception was that German policy must be guided solely by the direct and immediate self-interest of the German State. Such a policy is not only immoral, it is foolish and futile to the last degree. It ultimately produced the ruin of Germany. I believe it will always have this effect. You will not easily find men who are so far-seeing as to carry out a policy of

powerful nation, but it is a miserable doctrine for the smaller nations of the world. One of the objections to the League of Nations is that it threatens national independence. But what can be more disastrous to independence than for the small nations to be dependent on some stronger Power to save them from extermination ? The doctrine of anarchy and force is absolutely inconsistent with any real independent life, particularly of the smaller nations.

I think it is worse than that. If we are to rely on each nation enforcing what it thinks to be right, then each nation is made a judge in its own court. We in this country hold very strongly that it is vital for our tribunals to be absolutely independent of any prejudice in favour of one side or the other ; and to say that right and justice as between nations are to be enforced by each nation of itself is to make each nation a judge in its own court. Such a procedure produces, and will produce, disastrous results wherever it is tried. I do not wish to go into a politically controversial subject, but I believe that the failure to recognise the evil of this principle in the Treaty of Versailles and other Treaties is responsible for much of the unrest in the world to-day.

Above all, there is this fatal objection to the system of international anarchy. It makes justice and right dependent on the fortunes of war. We have in our own individual relations abandoned for centuries the idea that the ordeal of battle or duel is a satisfactory way of enforcing the claims of justice and right. We no longer think that the man who can fence most skilfully, or shoot the straightest, is likely to be right in his quarrel. It is just the same with nations. There is no ground for thinking that the nation which has had the best military training, and has spent the greatest amount of time and money and effort in constructing engines of destruction, is necessarily morally superior to the nations which have spent less. Therefore I do not think we need occupy further time in discussing whether international anarchy is right, for clearly it is wrong and disastrous in the highest degree.

A much more serious question now arises. Is there anything else to take the place of international anarchy? I am dealing with the moral aspect of things. I make no detailed reference to the destruction which will inevitably come upon the world unless we find some alternative; but I ask you, purely from the point of view of moral right, to consider whether it is really true that there is nothing else we can put in place of this doctrine of the strong arm.

I agree that it is a very difficult matter to construct any organisation of the nations comparable to the organisation of individuals in States. I do not think it is practicable to create a Super-State which shall have such overwhelming strength behind it, that apart from other agencies, by mere force, it can compel the obedience of all the nations to its commands. I believe that this is impracticable, and I think at present any attempt to establish it would be disastrous. But I am not sure that we ought not, in passing, to sound a note of doubt as to whether in the end it is true that the basis of a State depends upon its overwhelming force, or whether it is not much more true to say that it depends on the general agreement of the whole of the inhabitants of the State, that certain rules shall be obeyed by themselves.

I must assume, however, that the machinery of a Super-State is impracticable, and for the reason that it is impossible to construct any international organisation with overwhelming force, and with an authority that would command respect of all the governments who compose it. We must, therefore, look for something else, which will take the place of international anarchy on the one hand, and which will not go as far as the creation of a Super-State on the other. And I venture to believe that the experiment now being tried in the League of Nations is on the right line. That is to say, we aim at a universal agreement among the nations, to which all nations shall be committed in principle, working not by force, but by the operation of the public opinion of the world as the requisite sanction.

Undoubtedly public opinion is an enormous force, even among individuals. We speak of the police and the law as working by compulsion and force, but it is not really so. The great weapon of the law in a community such as ours, for example, is not physical coercion or punishment, but the disgrace which disobedience to the law brings upon the offender. That is what people really dread, and unless disgrace accompanies legal punishment, legal punishment has not a hundredth part of its effectiveness. That fact, every one will admit, lies at the basis of a great deal of the discussion which is now proceeding as to the value of slight or severe punishments. The truth is that, within limits—I am not dealing with extravagant cases—it does not much matter whether the punishment is slight or severe, provided it is one that conveys the moral reprobation and moral inhibition of society, and operates as a kind of moral ostracism upon the individual who suffers it. When therefore some great national feeling has removed from the government of a country its moral authority, as we have seen, I regret to say, in many countries, some of them quite near to us, then the law ceases to have the effect of repressing crime or of keeping order. Or again where, owing to the state of public opinion, a particular breach of the law is not regarded as disgraceful, then it is useless to send the offenders to prison. It does not deter ; it does not shock people. In some countries where it is illegal to sell intoxicating liquor, and where that illegality is not endorsed by the great mass of public opinion, it does not really operate as a great deterrent to send a man or woman to prison for a few days or a few weeks. And, in point of fact, we see it in another instance still more strongly. Any practitioner in the criminal courts will tell you that the great mass of people tried are people who have been convicted before. When I was sitting as Chairman of Quarter Sessions, four out of five of the persons who came before us were men and women who had frequently been in gaol before, and against whom therefore the element of disgrace no longer operated. They had lost their character. It meant little to them, from that point of view, and consequently gaol or punishment had no deterrent effect upon them. It is against the people who never commit crime that the law is strong, and the reason is because the disgrace attaching to conviction is very great. The public opinion of the great mass of the community is against lawlessness and crime.

This is the first thing to be achieved if we are to suppress war. At present war is not disgraceful among nations. It is not regarded as a crime. The only people who condemn it are the people who are beaten ; the victors scarcely ever condemn war, or if they do, it is under their breath. Until war in itself becomes disgraceful, we shall not get our organisation of public opinion, which is, after all, the great force on which civilisation depends. War is not yet regarded as a disgraceful thing because at present war is the only means given to the nations of enforcing right and justice. And since the combatants in a war always maintain that their side is just and right, and the only test as to which is just and right is success in war, it is evident that the successful country will never be condemned.

I found in America that many people believe the Covenant of the League of Nations to be defective because it does not condemn war with sufficient clearness and definiteness. There is in that country a movement for what is called the " Outlawry of War." I do not argue whether it is feasible and right in all its details, but its central idea is attractive. The first thing to do is to condemn war, to make it a crime, to outlaw it by some great international declaration to which all nations will agree.[1] There are practical difficulties in the way, but I believe that this movement proceeds from sound principles fundamentally. Our only real weapon against war is public opinion, and we cannot get public opinion to operate until we have established the broad principle that aggressive war is an international crime, and ought to be so regarded.

It is evident that if this principle is to be established we must provide for justice in some other way. We must make use of the force of public opinion, organised in such a way as not only to prevent war but also to secure justice. We cannot leave injustice unpunished, and wickedness triumphant among the nations ; and if we are to take away from them, as I think we must, the right to enforce justice for themselves, then we must give to them some other

[1] This is now in process of accomplishment by the Kellogg Pact.

means of securing that they are not subjected to injustice from others.

These two ideas—the effective prevention of war and the effective establishment of international justice—lie at the foundation of the Covenant of the League of Nations, whether perfectly carried out by the Covenant or not. And they are really, so far as war is concerned, the root from which the central idea springs. The central idea of the Covenant is this : that we shall prevent nations resorting to war against one another until there has been every opportunity of settling the dispute by other means. That is to say, war is to be postponed until public opinion, properly organised and properly applied, has had an opportunity of settling the dispute.

I am not sure that this goes far enough. I believe it goes as far as we can go at this moment, until we have carried out another great international reform —the most urgent task now lying before us : and that is disarmament or the reduction of armaments. As long as we leave it possible for nations to accumulate masses of armaments, particularly as long as we leave it possible for them to enter into competition in armaments with one another, I believe it will be useless to hope that any international arrangements which we can make will prevent nations from using those armaments for their self-preservation or the enforcement of what they believe to be their just claims, in times of great national excitement, when they believe they are suffering from serious injustice or are seriously threatened by their neighbours. I believe that just as we never really succeed in securing a peaceful community until we can persuade the people to go about without arms in their hands, so we shall never secure a peaceful world until we can persuade nations to go about, at any rate, with no more arms than are necessary for the purpose of internal order and defence. And in the present state of international fear and suspicion, when every continental nation regards itself as in possible danger from one or more of its neighbours, it is impossible to expect them to lay down their arms, or even to retain them on a common plan, unless we provide for general protection from aggression by any one nation.

I do not, therefore, believe that we can hope immediately and finally to destroy all possibility of war ; but I do believe that in practice and as a practical matter, public opinion, properly organised and properly applied, is strong enough to safeguard the peace of the world, and to prevent international aggression. The League of Nations is based on this assumption. And its first principle is that before the nations fight they shall agree to a period of from six to nine months during which the causes of dispute shall be investigated before an impartial tribunal, and, above all, shall be investigated in public, so that the world shall judge. This is a matter to which I attach the utmost importance. The more I have to do with the affairs of the League, the more convinced I am that the greater the publicity, the greater the probability of the League's success.

And so far, let us take courage from the fact that, on the whole, the League is working well. I do not say that it has not made mistakes, or that its machinery is perfect, or that all the decisions and the settlements which it has produced are beyond criticism. I certainly do not say that they will not be criticised by one or other of the parties to the dispute. Indeed, it is obvious that they will be criticised by one, and probably by both, of them. But I do say that on the whole the machinery of the League has worked well, that, where it has been given a fair opportunity, it has produced peace, and, in the vast majority of cases, not only outward and external peace, but a real fundamental drawing together of the nations in dispute. In the best cases, it has actually, as far as we can see, obliterated the whole bitterness which existed before ; and in other cases it has, with very few exceptions, produced a real settlement which is likely to endure. And therefore I say that it works. And I am convinced that it will work. I believe that it requires only one thing to make it work in all cases, even in the greatest and most difficult cases : and that is, that people shall believe in it. I am not, I hope, an unpractical idealist. I would willingly be an idealist, but I do not want to be an unpractical idealist. I recognise that we must walk before we run, that Rome was not built in a day, and that all such other maxims of our forefathers are true and important. But we cannot stand still. We must either advance or recede. We must be cautious, but we must be prepared to take risks in situations which are serious, if not desperate.

In this connection I venture to point out the enormous importance of Article 11, which is perhaps the most typical of all the Articles in the whole Covenant of the League. It is the whole philosophy of the League in three or four lines. The Article declares that " it is the friendly right of any member of the League to bring to the attention of the Council or Assembly of the League any matter which threatens the peace of the world, or the good understanding of the nations upon which peace depends." That is to say, it is required that any difficulty or dispute shall be discussed openly before the world, in the atmosphere of the League, and in the Council or Assembly of the League. This means nothing less than the claim that these things shall be brought into the open and discussed before the bar of the public opinion of the world. I believe that this is the essential thing really requiring to be done even more than anything else provided for in the Covenant. And I believe further, that if such provision had existed in 1914, the world would have been spared an incalculable amount of suffering and waste.

This, broadly speaking, is the policy of the League. It is the only possible way of advance, and I believe

that it is practicable.   I am sure that it is immeasurably superior to international anarchy, which is the
only alternative.

In this sense the policy of the League is a policy
to prevent war.   So far, it is a negative policy ; and
a negative policy is not enough.   The negative
commandment, " Thou shall not kill " must be
completed by the positive commandment, " Love
one another."   Among nations it is not enough to
prevent war.   We must foster and encourage goodwill between the nations of the world, and bring it
into effective operation.

No political machinery can accomplish this.   It
is not within the compass of any Covenant, though a
Covenant may do something.   It is a moral question
which depends on other agencies far more powerful,
though far less manageable, than the machinery of
Conferences or Assemblies.   But still something
may be done.   We can create the atmosphere in
which such agencies can work.   We can encourage
international co-operation.   We can secure that
those nations which really desire international
brotherhood and goodwill among men shall have an
opportunity of carrying out their plans.   This part
of the work of the League seems to me to have been
hitherto successful.   The mere existence of the
Assembly is a great achievement.   The mere bringing together of representatives of all the different
nations and languages and religions into one room,
and asking them to sit down together and examine

world questions, not in the interests of individual nations, but as they affect the prosperity and progress of mankind, this, I repeat, is a great thing, and produces a great effect. Anyone who has attended the Conferences at Geneva realises the far-reaching effect produced by such meetings of the representatives of the different nations, gathering together and working for common objects.

I remember well the first Assembly, when the League began to have a real existence, and began to work for great causes. I remember when it began to consider what could be done to save the suffering populations of Armenia. It was not in any way the selfish interest of any nation represented there. It was a common altruistic object, and therefore it brought all the nations together, anxious to do their best. In the recent history of the League, and especially in its last Assembly, nothing has been more admirable than the joint effort made by so many nations to come to the assistance of Austria, not only because it was of value to this or that nation that Austria should not be allowed to fall into chaos, but because they felt the appeal of a nation in distress, and because they thought it was the duty of the League, as a League and as representing international opinion, to do its best to rescue a nation which was in dire straits and in danger of falling finally into the abyss. It was a great effort, and I believe it is going to be a successful effort.[1] But even if it failed, it

[1] The success has been complete.

has been a great thing that such an effort has been made.

There have been many other things in which the members of the League have worked together for common objects, recognising the great truth that the nations are far more interested in common objects than they are affected by diverse hostilities. The opium question, the release of prisoners of war, the attack on the white slave traffic, and a large number of other activities which are not so well known, but which represent valuable efforts of international co-operation, have made it possible for something like a spirit of international amity to exist; and no one who has attended the Assemblies at Geneva can fail to recognise that an atmosphere has been created there, in which international disputes lose their bitterness, and their solutions become possible without disaster or humiliation to either of the contestants.

What, then, is the conclusion ? It is this. The League can work. It has proved that public opinion and international co-operation are and have been weapons against war, and that peace can be secured by their means. And if this is so, if there is even a " one per cent. chance " of its being so, then surely to secure the success of the experiment is worth any effort that can be made. Nevertheless, I believe that there is much more than a " one per cent. chance." I believe that there is a reasonable certainty of success, if we, the people of this country and of other countries, really desire peace and mean peace.

This brings to light the real obstacle which the people of the United States feel to be in the way of their participation in European affairs. I found this feeling among them. They say, " You do not really desire peace and mean peace ; you are still training your men, quarrelling and fighting, heaping up armaments and making secret treaties. Convince us that you really desire to live at peace with one another, and we will consider in a very different light your suggestions of international co-operation with us." That is true. It depends on ourselves. It depends on this country and on other countries, and not on countries in the abstract, but on the individuals who make up those countries. What do they really want ? This is what they have to make clear to themselves. If they are not going to work at this task of international co-operation, if they are not going to make it a success, a new war is as certain as anything can be in human affairs. And what does that mean ? Who can doubt—if he gives it five minutes' thought, or one-tenth part of the attention which he gives to his own affairs —that new wars will mean the destruction of economic civilisation, that they will mean the loss of all the achievements of art and culture, and a return to the barbarism of the seventh and eighth centuries ?

And what more ? Can we doubt that with the

loss of all these material advantages we shall also have a deep moral degradation? Let us not be deceived by the splendours of courage and self-sacrifice which war brings forth. There is no evil, however terrible, that is not accompanied by good. Indeed, by the reaction which evil creates inevitably in human affairs, it may be said that it produces good. But war is none the less evil. Self-sacrifice is not the object of war. It may be, and often is, an incident of war; but the object of war is slaughter and destruction of the enemy, with as little loss to ourselves as possible. Individual acts of heroism are not the rule in war, but the exception, and the more perfect the machinery becomes, the less will such acts count. Bombing towns from the air, poisoning masses of the civilian population, torpedoing commercial vessels at sight, and blowing to pieces millions of the most promising young citizens of the enemy State—these are not elevating and ennobling pursuits, nor does history in the past show that they have had any ennobling effect. True, men are found—and let us rejoice at it—whose moral nature is so strong that they can pass through such experiences without injury, and be all the stronger for them; but we have no right to count on that occurring, and no true account of what happened when a town was bombed, or a country overrun, or a battle fought, will show that heroes, moral as well as physical, are the ordinary creation of war. Let us pursue without wavering our quest for peace, and since the League of Nations is the only alternative to war, let us not hesitate to labour with all our might to see that this great experiment in humanity receives the support of the peoples of all the nations of the world.

VIII

INTERNATIONAL ARBITRATION

(1928)

ONE of the earliest steps towards civilisation must have been the substitution of arbitral decision for violence as the normal way of settling individual disputes. It long preceded the acceptance of any written or definite law. The patriarch of the family, the chief of the clan, or the priest, dispensed what he considered to be justice without any authority except his conscience. Even the cadi under the palm-tree cited no rules of law or precedent. Those came much later, first in the form of tribal customs, then as the laws sanctioned by religion, and finally in the to us familiar form of statutory codes and recorded decisions. Even in relatively civilised times such as those of the early Plantagenets in this country, the chief concern of the ruler was to establish a system of justice, to secure the right of the national courts to adjudicate in every dispute. That was far the most valuable achievement of reformers like Henry II and Edward I. They saw that the great thing was to enthrone the rule of law, to substitute reason for force, discussion for violence. Individual injury was not only a wrong to him who suffered, but it was an offence against the State, nor was it to be justified because the aggressor had genuine cause of complaint. Forcibly to enter land in another person's occupation was a crime, even though the land belonged to the entrant. The mere prohibition of violence would have done little unless some other remedy had been provided. If a man was not to take the law into his own hands, the State—that is, his fellow-countrymen organised for the purpose— must see him righted. So that there were always two lines of advance. Force was forbidden, order was established, and at the same time the law was developed so that a remedy was afforded for every wrong. And it is worth noting that where for one reason or another the legal remedy was inadequate, that of force remained. Duelling is an instance in point. According to the barbarous conceptions of those times, an injury to a man's honour was not capable of being redressed by an appeal to the Courts. It could only be " wiped out in blood." No doubt the duel was in origin ordeal by battle. But it soon degenerated from that, and became a form of condoned murder—an institution of the Christian West to which Pagan Rome had no parallel.

While the process of taming individual violence was still in progress, civilisation was faced with the problem of groups of citizens organised as subordinate semi-sovereign bodies within the States. Sometimes they were mere fortuitous collections of men under some enterprising leader, formed for the purpose of obtaining the government of the country. Roman history is a long chronicle of such incidents. Sometimes the tendency was systematised, or the same result was produced by the gradual coalescence of independent clans or tribes. Whatever the origin of the groups, their actions were identical. They armed themselves in castles and other strongholds, and, where the central government was weak, engaged in proceedings which varied from brigandage to civil war. It was this disease which, aided by the necessity of maintaining large frontier forces available to ambitious generals for their private purposes, brought about the ruin of the Roman Empire.

Central Europe narrowly escaped the same fate. For decades and even centuries great territories were devastated by contending chieftains, and as much as two-thirds of their population was swept away by famine and sword. In this country we did not suffer so severely, but even here the Wars of the Roses kept the country in a turmoil for more than a generation. To us it seems incredible. But five hundred years ago this country was the prey of unbridled militarism as much or almost as much as China is to-day. No great principle was at stake. No important result was achieved. The leading barons armed their followers, defied the law, and fought till exhaustion and the advent of Henry VII put an end to anarchy.

It is interesting and may be instructive to note the

measures which he adopted. A good deal no doubt depended on removing the causes of disturbance by putting an end to the rivalry of the two Roses, and by administrative improvements. But the two reforms which directly attacked private war were the stern abolition of the system called Livery and Maintenance, by which the feudal chiefs were enabled to keep little standing armies on foot ; and the creation of the new Star Chamber court, of sufficient power and prestige to determine disputes in which great men were involved, and which up till then had been the excuse and sometimes the cause of civil warfare. In other words, he established for these petty powers a system of disarmament and arbitration.

It is no doubt true that the analogy between individuals and nations must not be pressed too far. The so-called international right of war is not quite the same thing as

> " the good old rule, the simple plan,
> That they should take who have the power,
> And they should keep who can."

But both of them result in anarchy, though the evils of anarchy are more glaring and more all-pervading amongst individuals than amongst nations.

It is therefore at first sight surprising that so little attempt has been made to apply to the extirpation of international anarchy the methods which have been so successful in dealing with individual anarchy. But the explanation is obvious. There has been nothing of recent years in the community of nations to take the place of the sovereign power in the government of individuals. On the contrary, each State has regarded itself as authorised and indeed obliged to enforce its rights by its own strength. What those rights may be has been considered a matter to be determined by the State claiming them, and if the claims are not admitted, then in the last resort the dispute must be settled by war—as far as war can settle anything. It follows that from the earliest times each organised nation has asserted an unlimited right to go to war whenever it conceived that it was in its national interest so to do. It is true that when the Roman Empire was established over the whole civilised Western world the *pax Romana* obscured or suspended the right of war within the Empire. That was a consequence of the extinction of the independent existence of other nations. It did not imply any abrogation of the right of war as the ultimate sanction of national claims—a right, indeed, constantly acted on by Rome itself. As the Empire broke up and its racial constituents recovered their sovereignty, they reasserted their right to settle their disputes by slaughter and devastation. It is true that some limit was placed on this right by the Papacy, but in practice this came to very little unless the temporal or spiritual position of the Pope was affected. Rome had practically no power to restrain even the most atrocious exercise of the right of one nation to make war on another in the course of an ordinary secular quarrel.

But the Papacy did foster a moral and religious opinion which regarded war between Christian potentates as in itself evil. It did not question the sovereign right of war, but it urged the feudal chieftains and their suzerains not to exercise that right against their Christian brethren. To give a non-Christian outlet for the martial proclivities of Christian princes was indeed one of the chief motives for the papal advocacy of the Crusades. But the Crusades in this as in other respects were a failure. Devils cannot be cast out by Beelzebub, nor will the lust of slaughter be diminished by indulging it even against Mohammedans. Still, the unity of the Western Church and the principles of Christian morality did encourage the growth of a public opinion hostile to war, at any rate to what was considered to be an unjust war. Shakespeare represents Henry V as consulting bishops on the lawfulness of his attack on France, and although the episcopal justification seems to us very thin, the admission that war needs justification is in itself something gained. The teaching of the Church had at least produced that result.

When the international power of the Pontiff was shattered by the Reformation, it was a natural development that Grotius should seek in a new science of international law some substitute for the control of international anarchy, however feeble and intermittent, which had been till then exercised by the Vatican. Grotius' system rested on the postulate of a law of nature embodying the elementary conceptions of right and justice, and it was on this foundation that the structure of international law as we now know it was built up. Much learned argument has taken place as to whether the word " law " is rightly applicable to regulations and understandings depending only on moral sanctions. But whatever may be thought about terms, there can be no doubt that international law has exercised a considerable effect on the relations of States to one another, and has induced them to seek a justification for their actions in its rules. Nevertheless, the right of war remained untouched, except that perhaps the possibility of disapproval by public opinion was a more regular if not a more efficient limitation than that exercised in older times by the Pope. The result was that in modern times, though statesmen might seek to establish a moral basis for declaring war, there was legally no limit to its use as an instrument of national policy.

When Bismarck was urging on the King of Prussia the desirability of seizing the Duchies of Schleswig and Holstein, he was quite unmoved by the King's objection that Prussia had not any right to the Duchies, only replying that it had been the tradition of the Hohenzollern House to extend its territories. And for his two other wars, that with Austria and that with France, there was little or no more substantial basis. As Clausewitz puts it, " War is the supreme instrument of national policy, whereby one nation imposes its will upon another." The wording is noteworthy in view of the Kellogg proposals. In short, might was right in international affairs, though some nations might attempt more or less sincerely to cover up this fact with a profession that their methods were in accordance with the highest justice. Even so there was no external control of the sovereign right of all independent States to go to war when they pleased. They might intend to govern their conduct by the principles of fair dealing and morality, but that was an act of grace and favour on their part—something to satisfy their own conscience and the public opinion of the world. Interference from a foreign source was intolerable, and even an offer of mediation was liable to be looked upon as an unfriendly act. It followed that any idea of international arbitration was until quite lately no part of international life, for arbitrations involved the submission of a dispute to some authority outside the disputants, and therefore admitted the conception in principle that the sovereign right of a nation to order its external affairs as it likes is to be limited by the decision of the arbitrator.

In spite, therefore, of Grotius and of his followers, anarchy was complete ; every nation did that which was right in its own eyes, with consequences which became increasingly unacceptable both to the conscience and the interests of mankind. Every one knows that proposals were repeatedly made to abolish war, and establish in its place some system of international justice. It was not, however, till 1794 that a definite application of the principles of arbitration was made to international affairs. In that year the celebrated Jay Treaties, which provided for the submission to arbitration of outstanding differences between the British Empire and the United States, were concluded. The experiment was so successful that it has been followed in a very considerable number of cases since that date. Indeed, there have been some four or five hundred international arbitrations, of which those in which Great Britain or America have been engaged are by far the most numerous. We have every right to claim that we have led the way in this great international reform. But its extent must not be exaggerated. Arbitration was applied to a number of particular disputes, most of them of a minor character. It proved to be an exceedingly successful device. Though the enforcement of the award was necessarily left to the sense of justice of the parties, there is, I believe, no instance in which the arbitration award has been ignored. In how many cases the dispute, if not submitted to arbitration, would have led to war no one can tell, probably not any considerable number. But the right of war remained unaffected. Arbitration was merely conceived of as an alternative to negotiations through diplomatic channels.

The next step was the conclusion of a number of general arbitration treaties providing not for the settlement of one special dispute or group of dis-

putes, but establishing arbitration between the
parties to the treaties as the normal way of dealing
with any controversy between them. But even in
these cases the right of war, though limited, was not
wholly abolished. It became the custom to insert
in the treaties a reservation of all questions affecting
the honour or vital interests of the parties.
Obviously that destroyed the chief value of the
treaties as instruments for maintaining peace.
Nations do not fight about what they consider to be
trifles. Even the most reckless of militarists will
not plunge their countries into war except for some
cause which they regard as vital to national honour
or well-being. If, therefore, those matters are
excepted from arbitration, it is obviously no longer
an alternative to war, but at the best an improved
way of disposing of international differences of minor
importance. It is not therefore surprising that
when proposals were made at the Hague in 1899
for setting up a general system of international
arbitration, Prince Bülow should have triumphantly
reported to his Imperial master :

" Scarcely more than the name is left, by reason
of the clause inserted on Germany's demand,
whereby compulsory arbitration is debarred in all
instances where the vital interests or honour of a
State are affected."

If, therefore, agreements for general arbitration
are to be worth anything, this reservation must be
omitted from the treaties. This has been done in

our own treaty with Uruguay, and in a number of treaties, such as those between Argentine and Chile, Holland and Denmark, and Italy and Denmark, and others of minor importance from the point of view of world peace.

Parallel to this gradual development of international arbitration, there was in progress up to the outbreak of the world war a movement towards some kind of organisation of the civilised nations. It was fitful; springing into considerable activity at the close of every considerable war, and then gradually dying away when peace was restored. The old distich—

" The devil was sick, the devil a monk would be ;
The devil was well, the devil a monk was he "

is as true of nations as of individuals. Still, the movement went on from the days of the great design of Henri Quatre and the proposals of William Penn to the Holy Alliance of Alexander I of Russia. Even the disheartening failure of that effort did not arrest the movement. On the contrary, right through the nineteenth century, scheme after scheme was brought forward, sometimes by governments, more often by private individuals.[1] They failed of adoption, but their failures laid the foundation for later advance. The institution of war was undermined. Its rational basis was destroyed. Its inevit-

[1] A specially interesting scheme called the " United States of Europe " was brought forward in November 1916 by Sir Max Waechter.

ability was challenged. Statesmen—even those most averse to revolutionary change—began to look forward to a time when some kind of organisation of the peoples of the world would take the place of the existing international anarchy with its perpetual menace of international chaos. Thus Lord Salisbury in 1897 said :

"The one hope we have is that the Powers may gradually be brought together to act in a friendly spirit on all questions of difference which may arise, until at last they shall be welded in some international constitution which shall give to the world, as a result of their great strength, a long spell of unfettered and prosperous trade and continued peace."

Against these signs of enlightenment must be set one deep and growing shadow. The peoples were moving towards peace, but the governments of several of the more important States were moving towards war, and unluckily the most powerful Continental government of all, that of Germany, led the movement. It is not necessary to think that the German Emperor and his advisers consciously desired war. Some of them may have done so, but my own opinion is that the German Emperor did not. It was the military machine, the vested interests, material and moral, of the Army and the Navy that were fatal to peace. The competition of armaments, defended to the peoples as the only security for peace, made war unavoidable. Not only did the armaments create an atmosphere of ever-growing international suspicion, the very stuff that the war mind feeds on, but the burden which they imposed on the peoples, both in money and service, was so oppressive that a whole system of war propaganda had to be kept going to procure their acceptance. Some of it still survives in the great military and naval spectacles, the brilliant uniforms, the martial music, designed to excite admiration for the fighting professions and " to help recruiting." But before the war, in Germany and her imitators, a much more active campaign was carried out. Professors taught the glory of violence, the contemptibility of gentleness and self-sacrifice. Soldiers were instructed to look forward with longing to the " day " when they would once again march to victory. In the meantime they were given special privileges. Civilians had to give way to them in the streets and places of public resort. Their actions were not cognisable in the ordinary courts. Almost any form of violence was justifiable if it could be defended on military grounds. Above all, the Emperor and his lieutenants decried pacific methods of international discussion, and blustered about " mailed fists " and " shining armour." In other words, war was acclaimed as an instrument of national policy, and so long as that is the case, arbitration can at best be nothing more than a substitute for diplomatic negotiation. It can never take the place of war.

The position then, in 1914, was something like this. There had been growing for the previous

century a strong anti-war sentiment. Among most
people, certainly among most Englishmen, war was
regarded with repulsion both for its cruelty and its
futility. It was recognised as belonging properly to an
earlier stage of civilisation, to be indeed a " method of
barbarism." At the same time, international arbitration, though disliked by diplomats and militarists,
had been coming into popular favour. Arbitrations
were increasing, and arbitration treaties were multi-
plying. Attempts had been made, of which the
Holy Alliance and the Concert of Europe were
examples, at international organisation, but they had
not gone very far, and the efforts to make a more
substantial advance at the Hague in 1899 and 1906
had on the whole been disappointing. Moreover,
the old tag *si vis pacem para bellum* was still widely
regarded as expressing the highest wisdom, though
it brought in its train those " bloated armaments "
which all reasonable people—at least in this country
—regarded as an ever-increasing danger to peace.

One other observation should be made. Of all
the European peoples, the British most hated war.
They are a courageous people and not very imagina-
tive. They hated war but they did not fear it. It
did not seem to them real enough to bother about.
Lord Roberts failed to convince them that granted
that war was coming, it was better to prepare for it ;
and Mr. Norman Angell was equally unsuccessful
in persuading them that because war was futile and
wicked, vigorous efforts should be made to avoid it.

It must be remembered that for two generations we had had no real experience of war. Even the Crimean War had been fought in a distant corner of Europe, and though its horrors had for the time stirred the public mind, it had touched too small a fraction of the population to produce any lasting effect. The Boer War had not only been remote, but it had been fought without passion and with a minimum of cruelty and slaughter. Such indignation as it excited was chiefly political, and the agitation about the concentration camps—the " smoking hecatombs of slaughtered babes," or, more prosaically, the well-intentioned but only partially successful efforts to save the lives of enemy mothers and children—and the like, burned fiercely for a time and then died away. The result was that to most of us war was an unreal thing. We hoped that gradually arbitration would take its place, and that in any case if war occurred we should somehow or other be able to keep out of it. The same kind of feeling is already growing up again in the more placid official quarters.

Then came the War. In a month all our illusions were gone. We knew war to be as terrible as it is cruel and wasteful. And it went on for four years, while the tale of suffering and sorrow mounted up to heights before unimagined by the worst of pessimists. All the time it became clearer and clearer that though some international questions might be solved by the war, others would be raised not less

difficult or dangerous to the peace of the world.   So
the conviction grew that it must be the last war, that,
come what might, some less irrational, less intolerable
method of disposing of international disputes must
be found.   No one who remembers the reception
of President Wilson in London will doubt the depth
of that conviction.   It was not his courage or his
eloquence or force of character that brought those
vast multitudes of cheering men and women to greet
him in the streets of London, of Paris, of Rome.
The welcome was not to the man but to the idea of
Peace.   He was for the time the incarnation of all
that we most passionately desired.

And so the representatives of the nations went to
Paris and there forged the new instrument of Peace,
the Covenant of the League of Nations.   What did
it do ?   Well, it did several things.   Firstly, it
supplied what Lord Salisbury had pointed out in
1897 was essential to enduring peace among the
nations.   It set up a central, international organisation, the chief object of which was to prepare and
preserve the peace of the world.   That was probably its greatest practical achievement.   Next, the
Covenant laid down the new principle that peace
is the interest of all nations, and that therefore it is
the right and duty of each of the members of the
League to call to its attention any circumstance that
directly or indirectly threatens peace.

Then it provided that all disputes likely to lead to
a rupture, whatever their nature and whether they

affected the honour or vital interest of the parties or not, must go either to arbitration (including in that term a decision by the International Court of Justice, the establishment of which it directed) or to discussion by the Council. By a further provision no war was to take place until three months after the conclusion of the arbitration or the discussion before the Council, which might last not more than six months ; and if the Council were unanimous there was to be no resort to war at all against their decision.

The members of the League further agreed that they would refer to arbitration disputes which they recognised to be suitable for that method of procedure, and they declared that certain classes of dispute which may be called legal, such as questions about the interpretation of a treaty, and the like, were generally suitable. But they refrained from binding themselves absolutely so to refer such disputes, and it is generally considered that they are free to do so or not as they choose.

Lastly, it was recognised that the reduction of armaments was essential for peace, and the Council was directed to formulate schemes for the purpose.

It will be observed that the right to war remains in one case, namely, where a dispute likely to lead to a rupture has been referred to the Council, and the Council have not given a unanimous decision upon it. That is the celebrated " gap " in the Covenant, not perhaps of great importance from the point of view of the number of cases likely to come within it, but of considerable psychological moment. So long as the right of war remains, nations will evidently go on preparing for its possibility.

Secondly, disputes not likely to lead to a rupture are not completely covered. If they are not legal, indeed, no provision is made for their determination. If they are legal, arbitration is recommended but not made compulsory. On the other hand, the creation of the Court of Justice, which is directed by the Covenant and which was accomplished in 1921, was a great step forward. The mere existence of such a Court is a perpetual witness to the desirability of settling international disputes by justice rather than by force.

Finally, as in Arbitration so in Disarmament, though the line of advance is indicated, and the members of the League are pledged to follow that advance up, that is as far as the framers of the Covenant felt it possible to go in 1919.

Since the framing of the Covenant some considerable steps have been taken besides the erection of the Court. In the first place, by the instrument or statute by which the Court was brought into existence, an opportunity was given for those nations who were keenest for the general pacific settlement of disputes to make a further advance in that direction. This was the famous Optional Clause, which is a protocol attached to the Statute of the Court, open for signature by all those who adhere to the Court, which provides in substance that such as agree to it will accept compulsory arbitration in legal disputes with any other signatory to the protocol. Some twenty-seven States have already signed this protocol, and some fourteen or fifteen of them have ratified their signature.

In the second place, there were the Washington Treaties of Disarmament, which at any rate began the work of limitation of naval forces by international agreement.

Then came the Locarno Treaties. They were important because they dealt with a particularly difficult region in Europe, namely, the frontiers of Germany on East and West. In essence they were an application to a particular case of the principle of the Covenant. That is to say, they provided for the pacific settlement of all frontier disputes, with an extra provision that in case either side attacked on the Rhine frontier, all the signatories of the Treaties, including ourselves, would combine against the aggressor.

It will be noticed that there is no gap here. War between France and Germany is absolutely forbidden, and the sanction or guarantee into which we and others have entered has no reserve ; it comes into force the moment aggression takes place. Further, there is an absolute agreement to refer all legal disputes between the principal parties—not including the guaranteeing Powers—to arbitration, together with an undertaking that even with respect to political disputes they shall be referred to the League Council, and there is to be no war, even if no settlement is arrived at.

In the last few months we have had another proposal, more important than any which has been made since the Covenant was drawn up. It is the suggestion that a Convention should be signed first by the Great Powers and then by as many other countries as possible whereby war between the signatories should be absolutely and entirely renounced. It is explained that this would not preclude a signatory from defending itself, since if it were attacked by a co-signatory the latter would have already broken the Convention, which would therefore cease to apply. It is thought by some that difficulties may arise with respect to the operation of the Covenant against a Covenant-breaking State, but, since that is not the intention of the proposers, I will not further discuss the point here. Unquestionably it is very much to be hoped that the American Peace Pact will be generally agreed to. Its value, particularly its psychological value, would be of great importance. For the first time the right of war would be eliminated from international relations.

The obvious weakness of the plan is that it has no machinery for its enforcement. For instance, the right of self-defence remains in case an attack is made, but who is to say whether an attack has taken place ? Each country apparently is to judge for itself. Moreover, a threat of war, if it is clear and insistent, is just as much a use of war as an instrument of national policy, which is forbidden by the American Pact, as an actual physical aggression. Suppose a Continental Power assembles a great army on the frontier of another Power. Would that not constitute a breach of the undertaking not to use war as an instrument of national policy ? And if it did, would the other nation be free from its obligation and entitled to take measures of self-defence ? If, on the other hand, a country pretending to be threatened took aggressive measures against its neighbour, it then would be the aggressor. Yet there is no machinery proposed in the American plan for dealing with this situation. This is not indeed a serious criticism as far as members of the League are concerned, because the League machinery for determining whether aggression or resort to war has taken place could be used to decide who had really broken the American Pact. But with respect to countries which are not members of the League, the want of such machinery shows that, though of great value, the American proposals are not complete.

Meanwhile, the League has been making long-continued efforts to solve the problems of disarmament. I will not attempt to recount them here. It is enough to say that in the spring of 1927 a skeleton draft treaty was debated by the appropriate Committee of the League. No final conclusions were arrived at on some points, but the general outline of the Treaty was laid down and a good many difficult questions were solved. Certainly enough was accomplished to show that there was no impossibility in reaching a conclusion on this stage of the work. But that, of course, leaves unsettled the much more difficult question of determining the actual amount of the armaments to be accepted by the parties to any such agreement. Personally I am convinced that you will never get a complete and effective disarmament treaty unless the question of Security is tackled. Continental countries, that is to say, will never lay down their arms or even seriously diminish their armed forces unless they are satisfied that if they do so they will be protected from sudden and treacherous attacks from their neighbours. I remember very well in the meetings of the Disarmament Committee last spring feeling much oppressed by a certain sense of unreality caused by the refusal of the representatives of many of the Continental States seriously to tackle the problems before them till they knew how they stood with regard to Security.

That difficulty apparently remains. I believe it can be removed if one of the Great Powers were prepared to give a really vigorous lead in that direction, but so far no Great Power has done so. Each and all of them are too much under the sway of their technical advisers to make a real offer to collaborate in the cause of Security in return for a serious movement towards Disarmament.

Something no doubt has been done. The provisions of the Covenant have been clarified, at any rate so far as they deal with the prevention of war ; and an offer has been made of financial assistance for a country that is attacked without justification. But the efforts made have been so far without much response. The truth is that the war mind is undoubtedly far too prevalent in Europe at present. The problem is largely psychological and not material. Indeed, the real value of a big movement towards Security would be its psychological aspect, and I have no doubt that that result can be facilitated by other means, even without an offer of direct material assistance.

That is one reason why an advance in the direction of international Arbitration becomes of such enormous importance. Curiously enough, the Continent is more ready for such an advance than we are. That is partly due to the greater urgency of the danger of war, and partly to the fact that the writers of international law have more authority in Continental countries than they have here. We in our legal system care little for what jurists, however eminent, may have written. We rely exclusively on Statute Law and on judicial decisions as the sources of our legal rules. But on the Continent it is not so. The Continental jurists, indeed, pay little attention to judicial decision but a great deal to the principles laid down by writers of authority. And since almost all writers on international law have advocated

Arbitration as a substitute for war, the great body of expert opinion on the other side of the Channel favours an advance in that direction.

It is perhaps natural, therefore, that our Government should be displaying greater reluctance to accept arbitral settlement of international disputes than is common abroad.   We are told that public opinion would not support so great a change.   I can only say that all the evidence as it appears to me is against this contention.   Two great Parties in the State are pledged to it, and of the third a very considerable section is of the same opinion.   Personally, I have no doubt whatever that if, even in the present House of Commons, the matter were left to a free vote, there would be an immense majority in favour of such a step as signing the Optional Clause.

Then we hear it said that the obligations of our vast Empire are so great that it would be rash to bind ourselves to submit any dispute to Arbitration, and the case of the Venezuela Arbitration is cited in support of that view.   In that case, the British Government did not accept arbitration until the principles upon which the arbitration should proceed had been settled.   No doubt it was very desirable to get those principles laid down, though, as far as I can understand what was secured, it was little more than that the ordinary principles of international law governing such disputes would be applied.   Now that you have established an International Court of Justice which on the whole commands the confidence of the vast mass of opinion throughout the world, it is clearly unnecessary to take such great precautions as would be proper where an *ad hoc* tribunal had to be constituted, which may be more at the mercy of political considerations. But let us put the case at its worst : assume that another case like the Venezuela case arose and went to the Court without any limitation. And assume again—a grave assumption—that the Court decided wrongly and gave to Venezuela a larger tract than she was entitled to, thereby transferring, it may be, British subjects from British territory to Venezuelan soil. That would be unfortunate. It might even expose the British Government to the expense of compensation for the British subjects. It might even cost them a few thousand pounds. But that seems to be the limit of the injury we should suffer—surely a bagatelle compared with the advantage of getting established the principle that international disputes of a legal character must be settled by law.

So, too, I have heard people express anxiety lest we might be forced into arbitration over our position in Egypt, and be exposed to the possibility of a wrong decision on that subject. I think people who make this objection forget that in view of the line we have taken on this question it would be very difficult for us to resist a demand for international arbitration if the Egyptian Government were to make one. But I think it extremely unlikely that the Egyptian

Government would do such a thing, because I am myself quite confident that an international tribunal of reasonable competence would decide in our favour. But here again, even if an inconvenient decision were given, I am satisfied that the advantage to us of establishing arbitration would greatly exceed any such inconvenience.

The truth is, peace is essential to us. The very complication of our Empire emphasises it. The danger to our food supply in case of war, rightly stressed at Geneva last summer, cannot be overcome except by the preservation of peace. Any one, I am sure, who reads the debates which then took place will be satisfied that no amount of naval strength can be relied upon really to keep the ocean open to our commerce. Even if that were possible, it would not be sufficient, for we have now to protect ourselves not less from attack by air than from marine aggression. It is not that I am advocating concessions in order to buy peace. That I agree would never succeed. But to accept arbitration is not a matter of concession at all. It is, on the contrary, to establish and make secure one of the great principles of British foreign policy. We were the first of the European peoples of the world to establish the rule of law in our own land. We have maintained for decades, almost for centuries, that that beneficent sway should be extended to international affairs. No country has more constantly insisted on that proposition both in individual cases and in conferences. So far we have always been met with opposition by the great militarist nations of the Continent. For various reasons that opposition has dwindled away, and it would be a real tragedy if, at the very moment that the attainment of our long-desired goal was possible, we should allow a short-sighted timidity, and it may be an excessive deference to professional advisers, to rob us of a consummation so essential to the peace of the world and the existence of our Empire.

IX

THE FUTURE OF THE LEAGUE

(1925)

IT is a very great honour for me to have an opportunity of addressing an audience [1] connected with an institution which has always been in the forefront of progress, and has been marked in its career, now close upon a century old, by breadth of outlook and by that devotion to freedom and all the higher aspects of humanitarianism which are closely connected with the subject on which I am to speak to you to-night. I listened with respect and veneration to the list of names which were read out just now by your Chairman. They are men chosen from various walks of life of whom any university might well be proud. In particular there are two of them, the historian Grote and the Master of the Rolls, Lord Cozens-Hardy, whose acquaintance I had the honour to have, who might fairly be said to be men whose whole outlook on life was such that they must have been, had they lived in the time in which it was a fact—they must have been inevitably convinced supporters of the League of Nations.

[1] The University College Union Society.

181

But I am not here to speak to you to-night of the past or the great men of the past. I am here to speak to you of what already exists, and what we may expect it to grow into, the League of Nations, a subject of vital interest to all the world, and most of all to those who are still young. For, whatever may happen to us who are getting towards the end of our term of life, one thing is certain, that unless by the League we can prevent the recurrence of war, the outlook of the youngest of us is one of black despair; and I am here to speak to you to-night not so much of the League as it is, though I shall have to say something about that, as of the future of the League. And surely it is a great fact that we can now speak without any doubt about the future of the League. I think it is rather striking, if you throw your mind back eight or ten years, to find a great international institution organised for the maintenance of peace, of which we can not only say that it exists but, with all the confidence with which any human being can speak of any human institution, that it will continue to exist. It has, undoubtedly, a great future before it, and already one is able, in looking back to its comparatively short history, to wonder at the course which it has run in public estimation. I remember very well when it was being founded, when the average cultivated critic regarded it as a visionary and ephemeral institution, something born of the excitement of the war which would perish very shortly, something to be regarded with patronising favour but without any great interest. Then it became a little later a futile institution, which existed to enable a certain number of well-meaning but foolish persons to make speeches at Geneva. And then it became a very dangerous institution, one that threatened the liberties of the whole world. I remember very well reading in a pamphlet a passionate appeal against the League, on the ground that it was there to install that excellent and charming individual, Monsieur Léon Bourgeois, as the Dictator of Europe.

And now I notice a fresh development. The League is recognised, it is even grudgingly approved by its old opponents ; but it is told that it can only be of real service if it does not do anything very much. I do not know whether you remember the story of the gentleman who was asked what was the teaching of the Thirty-Nine Articles about Good Works, and he said, " The teaching of the Thirty-Nine Articles about Good Works is that a little of them won't do a man much harm." Whether that is a fair representation of that teaching I won't stop to enquire, but it is exceedingly like the attitude which certain people adopt towards the League of Nations at the present day. A little of it won't do the world much harm.

Well, all that is an entire misapprehension. The League is there. It has already proved its immense utility to mankind. It is growing in authority and importance every day, and I have not any doubt that unless some disaster occurs, it will achieve far greater services to mankind in the future than it has already achieved during its present existence. But the thing that I wish respectfully to impress upon you to-night is this, that we must not regard the League as a finished device, something which is now complete, and which we have merely got to see work. Like all human institutions it has got to grow or decay. I remember when the Covenant was first presented to the Plenary Conference at Paris, President Wilson in the speech presenting it, declared, " A living thing has been born." That is quite true. If I might venture to quote myself, which is always a mistake, I put it in a different way. My idea was the same, though not so well expressed. I said, " All we have tried to do "—I was speaking of the work of the Commission of the League—" is to lay soundly and truly the foundations on which our successors may build." That is the truth. The League must be regarded as something which is going to grow. If it does not grow it will disappear. We must not regard it as a complete institution, but it is of importance that we should try to see what are going to be its lines of development, and that we should recognise that its ultimate development must depend on the principle of growth within it. But it is also true, as I tried to show at Paris, that although the nature of its growth must depend on forces which none of us can control, yet each of us has a responsibility for trying to guide that growth into the most effective and beneficial channels. And if we want to realise how we can help most for the future, it is important for us to understand what is the direction in which the League is growing.

The League has three functions, corresponding to the three great functions of the government of a country. It has its legislative function, it has its administrative function, and it has its judicial function. I am not going to attempt to-night to give you a catalogue of its achievements in each of these departments, because, if you want to study the matter, there are many pamphlets and books which will tell you what it has done. The only thing that I think is worth saying about that is that in my experience its achievements are almost always under-estimated, that nobody seems to have any conception —or very few people, only those who are intimately connected with it—very few people have any conception of the immense variety and extent of its activities in international work. But that, as I say, is not my topic to-night. I want, if I may, to call your attention to certain symptoms and character-istics of this development in those three directions which I have mentioned.

Let me take the legislative aspect first. The great legislative organ of the League is the Assembly : that is the body which represents all the members of the League, and which meets once a year at Geneva. It is a very interesting body, and inter-esting to myself perhaps especially, because it is a case in which I am conscious that I was entirely wrong. I remember very well when we were elaborating the Covenant at Paris, I thought of the Assembly as a body chiefly of ceremonial value, something which would keep the League in touch with the nations which composed it, and which would be of some value, no doubt, as giving an opportunity for an annual statement of what the League had done, not a body likely to be of any great importance in the great international work that the League was to accomplish. Nothing can be farther from the truth. The Assembly has proved to be an immensely important body; it is the body of the League which really commands the respect of the whole world, and which no statesman and no government, however powerful, can afford to neglect, still less to despise. It is far the most important body, and I think you will have noticed that quite recently in the newspapers, when the Council of the League was considering the celebrated protocol of which we have heard so much,[1] they decided that they could not deal with the matter ; and that any decision on it, any conclusion that was to be drawn about it, must be referred to the Assembly ; and accordingly the protocol, with all the comments and criticisms that have been made upon it, will be considered and dealt with, no doubt, by the next Assembly at Geneva.

It is a curious body. On the face of it, if anyone

[1] The Geneva Protocol for the Pacific Settlement of International Disputes.

merely wrote an account of what it was, without knowing how it worked, they would say it could not possibly do any good. Because here is a body representing more than fifty nations, three representatives from each nation, which can arrive at no decision according to its constitution unless there is a unanimous vote of all the nations represented there. I venture to say that any reasonable commonsense individual—there are no people who are so often wrong as people of common sense—no ordinary man of common sense, would doubt that such an assembly as that could never arrive at any decision at all. As a matter of fact that is entirely untrue. I do not think there is any case of importance where a decision has been prevented by the impossibility of obtaining unanimity. I believe the rule of unanimity on the whole has worked extremely well, subject to what I shall say about it in a moment. I believe it has made everybody realise that they have got to state their case in so moderate and conciliatory a form as will obtain the assent of all persons of goodwill. No doubt, if you think of it as a body resembling Parliament, where there are a certain number of people who are anxious to prevent anything effective being done, the Assembly could not do anything at all. But since it consists essentially of a number of representatives of nations who meet together for a common purpose, namely the purpose of preserving the peace of the world, and passionately anxious that that purpose should succeed, under those conditions the rule of unanimity is not bad but good.

But it is only right to say that, in practice, two very important modifications have already grown up in the rule of unanimity, and the fact that you see the constitution of the League being moulded and modified by custom is one of the proofs that it is a living organism. The two great modifications are these. In the first place, by a courageous and very successful ruling of the President of the first Assembly it was decided that when the Assembly was unable to reach a unanimous decision, then a vote of the majority would not be technically a decision, but would operate as a recommendation to the governments composing the League. The French word *voeu* was the word used ; I know no nearer translation than the word recommendation. That is really a very important decision because it means this, that except in a few vital instances, you can get something, which is almost as valuable for the purposes of the League as a decision, by means of a recommendation.

Let me give you an illustration. The government of Canada was very anxious to obtain a ruling from the Assembly that Article 10—an article which has been very much discussed—did not oblige any government, member of the League, to take action unless that action were assented to by the constitutional authorities of the country in question ; and they moved a resolution to that effect, which was discussed and debated at great length, and eventually was put to the Assembly. As a matter of fact, everyone in the Assembly but one nation, Persia, was prepared to accept the interpretation which the Canadian Government had urged. The Persian representative alone said that he was bound in the absence of instructions to vote against it. The result was that technically no decision was arrived at, but you had a recommendation which had the authority of all the nations composing the League except Persia ; and in practice an interpretation of an article of the Covenant with that authority behind it was almost as valuable as something which would be technically called a decision. So that, by this very interesting development of the constitution of the League, you do get over the difficulty as to unanimity where you can get a great mass of authority behind you. A single recalcitrant state does not in the great majority of cases prevent a result to the deliberations of the Assembly.

Then there is another interesting development. Everything that is to be discussed by the Assembly has a first discussion by a committee of the Assembly, and in the committees of the Assembly there is no rule as to unanimity, because they are merely making recommendations to the Assembly which the Assembly is free to accept or reject. Decisions therefore in the committee are by majority. But an understanding has already grown up in the League that unless there is some very exceptional reason the Assembly will accept a decision sent up to it by a

I am not saying that is the course which is pursued in every case. As we all know, it was not pursued in the last Assembly in the case of the Protocol; there the Assembly arrived at a decision without referring it to a Special Conference. I am not sure whether that method of procedure has turned out to be the wisest under the circumstances. Well, now, all this seems to me to show the principle of growth in the Assembly. I am convinced that this Assembly, representing all the Powers, members of the League, is likely to grow, and that the doubts and hesitations as to the League which have sometimes found favour, the belief, the fear lest it would develop into a second Concert of Europe, a mere collection of a few of the Great Powers, that fear will never be materialised as long as the Assembly exists ; because in the Assembly all Powers have an equal legal and constitutional right to be heard and to express their opinion, though, of course, some Powers are necessarily of greater influence than others. I believe that the Assembly is the great guarantee of the principle of the universality of the League, the principle which enables the League to boast, as Monsieur Briand said in a very remarkable speech he made the other day at the Council at Geneva, that it exists to further not only the legitimate interests of the Greater Powers, but also not least, and not less important, to protect the rights and privileges of the Smaller Powers as well.

That is the legislative side of the League. Then

there is the administrative side. There, as it seems to me, the progress has been very considerable but not nearly so complete. I am not sure that you can say that the League has, strictly speaking, any direct administrative functions. It does not direct administrative work by its own decisions immediately and without the interposition of any other authority. But it has a great many indirect administrative functions ; and those are all, or almost all, carried out by the Council—the smaller body representing the ten[1] Powers that have seats on the Council. There you will not find, as I say, direct administrative work. You will not find, that is to say, the Council ordering that such and such administrative action shall be taken in this or that case, or by this or that body. What you will find is this, a rather interesting and to some extent novel form of administrative action. You will find a number of administrative authorities who are subject to the League, in the sense that they were appointed by the League, and from which an appeal lies to the Council of the League. These exist and do administrative work, and the Council of the League is there generally to oversee their work, and particularly to decide on appeals or difficulties that are brought before the Council, where there is some fear of injustice or neglect having occurred.

The best known and most complete instance is the government of the Saar Valley. That, as you

[1] Now fourteen.

know, was a valley that was taken from Germany and put under a Commission which was appointed by the League of Nations. The Commission is an autonomous body. It has complete administrative power, but there is an appeal to the Council of the League ; which cannot indeed interfere directly in the administration but can make recommendations to the Commission, which in fact have a force of command ; because if the Commission refuses to obey them it is always in the League's power at the next opportunity to put an end to the authority of the Commission. But, strictly speaking, the Council does not have any direct administrative power. That is the nearest approach, as far as I am aware, to administrative action.

In other cases, such as the reform of the Austrian finance, what is done is rather different. A High Commissioner is appointed, who has charge of certain administrative functions. He reports at intervals to the Council of the League. The Council of the League does not interfere with him at all, but expresses at intervals its approval, disapproval or recommendation in respect of the work he is doing.

So still more in the case of the Mandates Committee, you have still greater absence of direct administrative authority ; because in that case the administrative authority is the Mandatory, which merely reports as requested by the Mandates Commission of the League what exactly it has been doing. On that report recommendations and advice are given, and suggestions are made ; but the authority of the Mandatory is absolutely complete and supreme, and it is only by means of public opinion and good advice that the administration by the Mandatory of the mandated territory is affected.

In all these cases, the administrative work of the League is far less complete than its legislative work ; and as far as I can see that must be so, as long, at any rate, as the Secretariat is constituted on the lines on which it is now constituted. It consists, as I am glad to be able to say with great conviction, of men and women of very great ability and absolute devotion to their work. But it is a smallish body. It is a very cheap body as administrative bodies go. As long as it is constituted on these lines it cannot do regular administrative work, and if at any time the nations of the world desire to place upon the League direct administrative work, then in my judgment they will have to increase both the numbers and the salaries of the Secretariat.

Now I pass for a moment to the judicial work of the League. Here we are perhaps on the most advanced ground of all the League activities. You have got now established a permanent court of justice, which is in all its procedure, all its methods and all its reputation as high as, or higher than, any similar court of justice in the world. Everything any of us thought about the advantages of a permanent court of international justice has been more than fulfilled. It has shown, as we hoped it would show

—by reason of the fact that it is appointed once for all and not to dispose of a particular dispute—it has shown a remarkable impartiality. It has been able to carry out its decisions—its successful decisions— with a continuity of thought which would have been quite impossible in an *ad hoc* body—or rather a series of *ad hoc* bodies—and it has in consequence achieved, even in its short career, a degree of authority which really is very little short of marvellous. I know of no instance in which its decisions have not been accepted with complete loyalty, whichever way it decided ; even where it was not strictly speaking a decision at all, but merely advice given to the Council as to how a decision ought to be made. In every case its decisions have been accepted, and the authority of the Permanent Court of International Justice, great as it already is, is growing every day of its existence.

There is a development of it which, I think, has escaped a good deal of notice, but which is exceedingly interesting ; and that is the development of what are called its Advisory Opinions. The Council, or for the matter of that the Assembly—it usually is the Council—is empowered to seek, in any case it likes, the advice of the Court on any question of law, or on any question which it thinks is suitable for the Court to give advice upon. The result is this : that if a dispute between two nations comes before the Council, and there is included in it any aspect which is suitable for decision by the Court, the Council is

empowered—and it is with increasing frequency
that it acts upon its power—to send that part of the
dispute, which may be in fact the very kernel, to the
Court for an Advisory Opinion. The Court gives
its advice practically in the same form as a decision ;
and when that Advisory Opinion comes back to the
Council it is, as I have already stated, practically
the same thing, or almost the same thing, as a decision
by the Court. Just observe how important that is.
It means that we have in effect the power of obtaining
—with or without the will and consent of the parties
to a dispute—the power of obtaining a judicial
decision on practically every International controversy ; very like compulsory arbitration, at any rate
in all arbitrable questions.   It is only subject to this
safeguard, that it must be such a question as the
Council of the League thinks is suitable for arbitral
decision.   It is almost an accident that that system
has been arrived at.   I confess it has to me very
great attractions.   It seems to me to procure a very
large part of the advantage of compulsory arbitration
under conditions and safeguards which make it
practically certain that that procedure will not be
in the future abused.

Now I think that if you take these three functions,
the relatively complete legislative function, the
relatively complete judicial function and the embryonic—I do not think you can say much more—
the embryonic administrative function of the League,
it really does look as if we were on the road towards

that Federation of the World of which poets have spoken, but which hitherto we have regarded as quite a visionary ideal.

But do not let me go too far. For there is one very important aspect in which the League falls short of anything in the nature of a government, as we understand government in the national sense. It has no coercive power. It is astonishing how in popular controversy that central fact about the League is so constantly overlooked. People say the League should compel, or should enforce on reluctant bodies some particular decision. It has no power to do that. That is not suggested as a power in the Covenant. All its powers consist in bringing the parties together to come to an agreement, to assist them by furnishing them with a judicial decision, to offer to them such facilities in the way of administrative action as may be suitable to the circumstances. But it has no power to compel any reluctant disputant, except the power of public opinion : it has no direct power of enforcing any of its decisions. I say that not forgetting of course the existence of the celebrated Article 16. Article 16 certainly has coercive force, but it is not coercive force set in motion to compel obedience to any decision of the Council or Assembly of the League. Article 16 says in effect—I am not quoting the words —that any country that resorts to war without having tried to settle its dispute by every other means, and without having given a sufficient period for reflection

and observation to the other countries in the world
—any country that resorts to war without fulfilling
these conditions is exposed to the severest international penalties, beginning with diplomatic rupture,
and going on to economic pressure and finally, if
necessary, military action. All that is comprised in
Article 16. But it is to enforce the submission of all
the countries to the procedure which will make for
peace. It is not to enforce a particular settlement
of any dispute, and that is a very important distinction. Article 16 is in my judgment a very important,
a very vital article of the Covenant, and I observe
that in the recent reply of the Council to the German
note about entry into the League—in which the
Germans suggested that they might be free from
some of the obligations in Article 16—the Council
in reply emphasised the immense importance of
Article 16 ; and on that ground amongst others
declined to favour any exceptional exemption from
the provisions of that Article.

It is perhaps worth pointing out in this connection
—though I am not going to discuss to-night the
merits or demerits of the celebrated Protocol of
Geneva—it is perhaps worth pointing out that in
that respect there is perhaps the greatest novelty in
that document ; because it did contemplate, with
very considerable safeguards no doubt, but it did
contemplate that decisions of an arbitral tribunal
under that document might be the subject of enforcement under the sanctions indicated in that document.

It proposed in that respect a very considerable change from the theory of the Covenant. Whether it would make a very considerable change from its practice is another matter, but it did mean a very considerable change from its theory ; because, as I have said, the great principle of the Covenant is that it promotes agreement and does not impose a settlement. I am inclined to think that the proposal of the Protocol is premature. I believe that before we take a step of that kind a great deal of progress is necessary in international public opinion. I have always believed that the first step to take is similar to that which we took early in our law, the establishment of the doctrine of the King's Peace, that every crime that is committed is not only a crime against the individual who is injured, but is also a crime against the whole of the community of which he is a member. We want that principle established and enforced in international affairs. We want it to be recognised that a country that wantonly makes an aggression against its neighbour is guilty not only of a crime against that neighbour, but a crime against the whole of the community of nations. That is the first fundamental principle, and until we can get as far as that I myself doubt very much whether it is possible to advance further. After all, we must recollect that the nations of the world are only just emerging from something very little removed from international anarchy ; a condition where every nation did what it thought right in its own eyes. We have got to get beyond that. We have got to get to the conception of an International Peace, which it is the higher interest of every nation to enforce and maintain ; so high that any breach of it, however distant, however apparently remote from any nation, is a great blow at its dearest and most important interests ; so that it will be prepared for that, and perhaps for that alone, to make any sacrifices, however great, in order to maintain the peace on which the whole of international life is ultimately founded.

That is the great conception that it seems to me we have to reach with all nations. And it is a conception that is making headway ; not perhaps so much in this country—I won't say that—not so vivid in this country as it is in some others. But I read the other day a speech made by the very distinguished and able Foreign Minister of Czecho-Slovakia, Dr. Benes, and in that speech he drew a moving picture of the condition of insecurity and danger in which the states of Central Europe necessarily existed, and made a great appeal that this insecurity should somehow or another be ended ; that they should be given a chance to live their lives in peace. And he pointed out, and surely it is true, that this is not a matter only for them ; that it is not a matter which only interests them, unless we have failed to learn the most elementary lesson of the late war, namely that a dispute right away in the south-east corner of Europe may be one which is vital to the interests of this country, and of all the other countries of Europe.

That seems to me to be the great advance, the great next step in the future of the League. Can we really get the nations of the world to understand that conception? After all, nations in time past have been content to struggle and make sacrifices, terrible sacrifices, for what they regarded as their own interests, their own vital interests. If they would only see it, there is no more vital interest than the maintenance of the peace of the world. That is an observation which will appeal naturally to those who are sometimes called Pacifists, those who believe already in the importance of peace. It is an observation which will appeal, I am convinced not less earnestly, to those who have never regarded themselves as Pacifists, who have always been ready in the last resort to make every sacrifice—the supreme sacrifice if necessary—in defence of their country and their country's interests.

I saw as I came in here a poster asking whether the League of Nations was incompatible with membership of the Officers' Training Corps? Certainly not. Who can think so who really understands what the League of Nations means? The League of Nations is not a convenient way of making life easier or softer than it was before. The League of Nations may, if we really grasp it, if we are really in earnest about it, demand from us just as great sacrifices as any other system; but they will be sacrifices not in the cause of national greed, or even in the cause of national honour, but in the cause of the peace of the world and the good of humanity at large.   I am convinced that the League of Nations has no warmer supporters than those who know what war really means, who have been taught by bitter experience what it is.   In this country the great organisations of the ex-service men are all for the League of Nations.   In France its strongest support is the great association of those who were mutilated, as they put it, in the Great War.   We may well say with Walter Scott that " war is sweet to them that never tried it."   It is not among those who know what war and real fighting mean, what trenches mean and all that trenches imply—it is not amongst those that you will find any lukewarmness in the cause of the League of Nations.   It is among those who have sat at home and written fiery articles in the papers, or made fiery speeches on the platform, or indulged in some other way in patriotic emotions under a system of limited liability—it is amongst those and those only that you will find blind hatred of the League of Nations.

I venture to appeal to you, ladies and gentlemen, you of the rising generation—it is your cause more than that of any other section of the community— are you going to grow up and do nothing to extirpate this great curse from humanity ?   Are you going to do nothing to protect your country from the greatest of all evils ?   Is your patriotism to be of so unseeing a character that you cannot perceive that peace is really and truly the greatest British interest, that it is an interest which calls for from you the greatest sacrifices and the greatest energy—sacrifices and energy which should have no limit except the successful achievement of the cause that you have in hand ?

X

THE LEAGUE—THE PRESENT POSITION
(1928)

EIGHT years ago the Council of the League of Nations met for the first time at Paris. Important personalities gathered round the table, but it is safe to say that very few of them believed in the importance or even the continued existence of the League. Indeed, it was the fashion at that time—particularly in the United States—to prophesy its immediate decease. Scarcely half a year passed without some triumphant declaration that the League was dying or dead. Nevertheless it has not only survived: it has done an immense amount of international work, which by the admission of everyone has been of great value. Mistakes have no doubt been made in its name. That is inevitable. But its chief danger is not that sometimes it will act wrongly, but that it may allow itself to be immobilised by the chancelleries of Europe. For every human institution must either grow or decay. It can never stand still. The activities which were sufficient to deal with the difficulties of yesterday must expand if they are also to solve the problems of to-morrow.

So far the League has scarcely tackled its most momentous tasks. It has improved international intercourse, it has struck some effective blows at grave social evils, it has rescued some hundreds of thousands of men, women and children from captivity or starvation, it has done something to restore the economic situation in Europe, it has succoured states floundering in a financial morass, it has procured the settlement of a certain number of international disputes and in one or two cases has prevented what seemed to be imminent hostilities. These are no mean achievements, but they come very far short of the object for which the League was brought into existence. For the chief end of the League is to destroy war. Unless and until that is accomplished its other work must be of relatively slight importance.

Now war is one of the oldest human institutions. To put an end to it means the reversal of a mass of understandings and assumptions, the destruction of a number of moral and intellectual—not to speak of material—vested interests. It has behind it a literature of its own. Poets and philosophers, novelists and historians have combined to sing its praises partly because it was the sport of kings, partly because of the heroism of those who have taken part in it, and partly because in the absence of some other means of obtaining international justice a state had no resource but war to secure its honour and existence against the fraud and violence of its neighbours.

Even so, and making all allowance for the splendid qualities it has called forth, it may well be doubted whether any other single cause has inflicted on the human race one tenth of the suffering which has accrued to it from war with its accompaniments of dishonesty, lust and cruelty.

The task of the League then is to destroy war— a task of enormous difficulty. It certainly cannot be accomplished at a single stroke or in a few years. It will need all our energies, all our courage and all our faith. The first step is to get rid of the notion that it is lawful for one nation to make war on another at its own will and pleasure. That step has been taken so far as all members of the League of Nations are concerned. It is implied in the Covenant and has been definitely expressed more than once in resolutions of the Assembly to the effect that " aggressive war is an international crime." Those resolutions only bind members of the League. If President Coolidge's proposal, that war as an " instrument of national policy " should be removed, is to be construed as in substance a proposal to extend to the United States a proposition of international morality already accepted by the members of the League it is much to be welcomed. But mere denunciation of war as an instrument of national policy will be by itself of little effect.

It is impossible to condemn wars really undertaken in self-defence. Nations cannot be expected to agree to submit to invasion. Yet the difficulties of defining aggressive war are great. In the late war every government professed to be fighting in self-defence. To prevent war the same steps must be taken by nations—in some rudimentary form at least—as were long ago taken in the case of civilised individuals. Private violence must be forbidden even to redress wrongs, courts where justice can be obtained and violence condemned must be established to protect the law-abiding, and there must be brought into existence something like an international police force, or if that be impracticable an international *posse comitatus*—that institution by which our ancient constitution laid upon all good citizens the duty to assist the sheriff in suppressing any breach of the Peace.

Above all, weapons of violence, armaments, in the hands of nations, must be reduced and limited to those necessary for self-defence and the enforcement of international obligations. A scheme with this purpose is now being elaborated by the so-called Preparatory Commission of the League, and a perusal of the verbatim report of its last session at Geneva is in many respects encouraging. It is the record of a business-like body—a body which cordially endorsed Lord Cushendun's well-timed appeal for definite action. Partly in consequence of that appeal, three *rapporteurs* have been appointed to prepare proposals for arbitration, guarantees of security and the explanation or precision of the Covenant. That is all to the good. But there is one danger against

which it is of the utmost importance that the government should be prepared.   There are not wanting
those who believe that the whole of these proceedings
with regard to security and arbitration are designed
only to evade actual limitation of armaments.
Critics of this school think that the idea is to bring
forward some suggested scheme of security which is
not acceptable to all the Powers concerned.   When
it fails it will then be said that disarmament is
impossible without security, and since security is
refused disarmament must also be dropped.   We
may confidently believe that our government would
not countenance any such manœuvre for a moment.
But they must take great care not even to appear to
connive at it.   Lord Cushendun has asked very
properly for a definite scheme of security.   When it
appears he must not be instructed to turn it down
lock, stock and barrel.   That is what the British
Government did in the case of the Treaty of Mutual
Assistance.   They did it again in the case of the
Protocol.   In both cases a proposal for which the
British Representative was largely responsible was
summarily rejected by the Home Government.   If
it happens a third time in the case of these new
proposals when they are made it will be at least
plausible to fasten on the British Government the
responsibility for stopping International Disarmament.   That would in itself be serious enough, for
our national prestige depends at least as much upon
character as upon strength.   But apart from the

effect such an event would have on our national position, its direct consequence must be of the utmost gravity.

We and other Powers are under perfectly plain and explicit obligations to our late enemies, and especially to the Germans, to proceed with a general reduction and limitation of armaments. It was on the faith of these promises that the Germans, as they allege, agreed to their own disarmament. Whether or not the two obligations are verbally dependent on one another, it is obvious that it will be impossible to insist on the maintenance of German disarmament except in return for a general and serious step in that direction by the other great European Powers. Count Bernstorff has recently pointed this out at Geneva and no one has traversed his contention. It is clear therefore that if the present policy at Geneva fails the Germans will claim to re-arm. That means the end of international disarmament and almost certainly the abrogation of those advances towards European goodwill so laboriously achieved at Locarno and elsewhere. It would be indeed a terrible responsibility for us if it could be said with any truth that our action had contributed to such an overwhelming disaster.

XI

DISARMAMENT AND THE LEAGUE[1]

(1923)

In the first place, let me tender to you my warmest thanks for the kindness of your welcome, for this fresh proof of the hospitality, so world-famous, of the American people, and above all, let me thank the Foreign Policy Association for the extraordinary success with which this gathering has been organised. It is, I am sorry to say, the first time that I have had the honour of visiting this country, and it is a matter of profound pride and gratification that I should at last, after many disappointments, have the opportunity of saying something which possibly may be of use and of hearing something which I am satisfied will be greatly to my profit in intercourse with a great audience like this.

I have many reasons for gratification at this opportunity. I am not one of those who have forgotten the comradeship of our two peoples in the great war. I shall never forget as long as I live that thrill of joy and happiness with which I heard the

[1] Address delivered before the Foreign Policy Association, Hotel Astor, New York.

decision of the American people to take their part by the side of the Allies in that great struggle.

I shall always remember the thrill with which we watched the first battalions of American troops marching through London ; and I shall never forget, nor will any of my fellow-countrymen, the glorious deeds and magnificent services which the American army rendered to our common cause in those critical days of 1918. I remember very well that my happiness—our happiness, I think I may say—was not only for the immediate assistance which you gave to us, but because we saw the dawn of a new era in which our two peoples should march together in the cause of peace.

There have been, as Mr. McDonald has already said,[1] many disillusionments and discouragements since the armistice was signed, but I for one have not abandoned, and will never abandon, the hope that the great work of peace will ultimately be accomplished by the joint effort of the American and British peoples.

There have been quite recently, if you will allow me to refer to it, some circumstances which have greatly heartened and encouraged those who think as we do. I rejoice profoundly that we have settled and put out of the way that difficult question of the debt, and I am not less, not more, thankful for what I may call the straightforwardness of our represen-

[1] James G. McDonald, chairman of the Executive Committee of the Foreign Policy Association.

tative, Mr. Baldwin, and his colleagues, than for the generosity of the American negotiators who met them and concluded that great arrangement. It is one of those arrangements like the quality of mercy, " it blesses him that gives and him that takes," and its greatest virtue lay not in the particular terms arrived at, though I have no criticism of them ; it lay in this, that it was the first great liquidation of the economic position left by the war, and furnished a great example to other nations of what ought to be done if we are to reach a real condition of peace.

That is not the only instance, by any means, of co-operation between our two countries. There were just about a year ago completed the negotiations which resulted in the Washington Treaty of Disarmament. That was a very great thing. It was a concrete achievement in the cause of peace. It is quite true it applied necessarily only to naval matters, and was in the nature rather of a limitation than a reduction. It is quite true that it applied only to capital ships ; and there are many I should imagine, certainly you and I in this room among them, who would have been very glad if it could have gone even further than it did. For our part, at least for my part, I should rejoice greatly if we could have a similar limitation, not only of capital ships, but of submarines and other craft also.

All warfare is cruel and horrible, but in naval warfare I do not know anything which is more cruel and more horrible than the hidden attack of the submarine, made without warning, made without discrimination, an attack which may send to their death not only the troops and combatants, not only the men of the opposing party, but women and children also. It seems deplorable that when we came to limit naval armaments, we could not limit the worst and the cruellest of all those armaments. I do not forget that regulations were agreed to which would make that form of warfare more humane. I am very glad they were made, but I should deceive you if I pretended that any regulations for humanising warfare were really likely to be of great value. War is a horrible and devilish thing, and when nations under the stress of that experience are at death grips with one another, when their whole future and existence depend on the result of the struggle, it is too much to expect that any paper regulations will limit or humanise the means which they employ ; and if we doubted it, the experience of the late war is a terrible warning to those who think that there is any means by which you can make war more tolerable. The only thing is to prevent its happening ; that is the only security for humanity.

In addition to naval disarmament, perhaps more urgently even than that, we require ultimate disarmament, immediate reduction in armament, both by land and in the air. After all, in many ways, land armaments are more destructive to peace, more dangerous to humanity than armaments by sea. You cannot invade a country with a fleet. That can only be done by infantry. You cannot make—at least, it is not very easy to make—a sudden and unforeseen death stroke at the life of a country by a fleet. That is the work of a land army attacking without provocation and without warning.

And if that is true of a land army it is even more true of the air. You know—we all know—that in the last war attack from the air was for the first time made a practical part of warfare. We all remember —we at any rate on the other side of the Atlantic remember—what bombing from the sky really meant. We have a vivid recollection of great explosives falling indiscriminately in the most populous and peaceful of our cities, slaughtering without discrimination every kind of human being, destroying the most harmless and the most helpless just as readily as those who were fighting in the field. What was done in the late war is but a pale shadow of what will be done in future wars. I am told that already bombs exist one hundred times as powerful and destructive as any that were used in the last war, capable of destroying great areas. And it is not only destruction that is threatened but poison as well. A bomb may be dropped from the sky on a great city. It may level large areas of it to the ground. It may poison the whole of the population for, it may be, miles around the place where it falls. Nor does even that exhaust the possibility of air attack. There are some human beings who are planning, I am told, that you should be able, not only to poison, but to kill by disease the population by bombing from the air.

Nor will any country be safe, for just as the extent of the damage to be done has grown enormously, so also has the range of attack ; and it is no wild idea that in the near future it will be as easy to send aeroplanes across the Atlantic as it is now to send them across the Channel. This, if it stood alone, would be surely a strong call to the peoples of the world to set their house in order, and to make a determined effort to limit these agencies of destruction before it is too late.

But do not misunderstand me. I do not wish to belittle what was done at Washington. It was a splendid achievement. It was a magnificent step on the road which we all wish to follow, all the more desirable, all the more admirable, because it was the first step ; and we know from the French proverb that it is the first step that is really difficult. But when we take the first step let us ask, where is that first step going ? What is the position we have now reached ? In my judgment, we have come to a great crisis in the history of humanity. I agree with what my countryman, Lord Grey, said the other day : " The nations must learn or perish." That is the truth ; that is the dilemma ; that is the issue that is laid before all of us, wherever we live, whatever our station in life, whatever our political or social aspirations.

I had the honour of crossing the Atlantic in

company with a number of your fellow-citizens who
were returning from a visit they had paid to Egypt
to see the marvellous discoveries which have been
recently made in that land. They spoke to me with
interest and enthusiasm of the astonishing degree to
which the ancient civilisation of Egypt had been perfected. There were others who had been to Crete
and who told me the same story, that the ruins and
remnants of Crete show an extraordinary degree of
civilisation in that land four or five thousand years
ago. And yet those civilisations, so advanced, so
perfected, had so completely disappeared that it is
only the work of scientific observers in the last few
years that has brought to light any trace of their
existence. Or take the case of Rome. I agree we
know more about Rome than we do about Egypt and
Crete. But I do not think that it is realised how far
Roman civilisation had advanced. I was told the
other day that when in 1835 the English minister,
Sir Robert Peel, was summoned hastily from Rome to
create a government in my country he took precisely
the same time, no more, no less, that a Roman
emperor would have taken in performing the same
journey 1700 years before.

Yet the Roman civilisation perished, barbarism
recovered possession of the whole of Europe, and the
condition of my country and of the greater part, if
not the whole, of European countries, relapsed so
that that civilisation became a mere dream and
memory. It is said often that Rome perished by

reason of the invasion of the barbarians round her
borders. There is no truth in that delusion. Rome
perished because the sections and nations which
made up the Roman Empire were unable to keep
from fighting with one another ; they destroyed the
Roman structure, and the barbarians merely came
on to the scene of the crime after it had been committed. Rome committed suicide. Let us take care
that our civilisation does not commit suicide also.

And if we are to work for real peace, an established
peace, be well assured that we have no security for
its permanence unless we succeed in limiting and
reducing the armaments of the world. There is no
use to hope that there is any real security for permanent peace so long as the nations stand on one
side or the other of their borders armed to the teeth
for aggressive warfare. Every one agrees to that,
not only in this country but practically all over the
world. There is no dissenting voice ; they all say
that armaments should be reduced ; and yet at this
moment no reduction has taken place in the aggre-
gate. Some of the great nations have reduced to
some extent their numbers from just before the war,
but other great nations, and other nations not so
great but just as warlike, called into existence by the
peace, have each insisted on their armed establishment, and in spite of the fact that Germany has
very largely been disarmed, I am told that the net
amount of armed men in Europe is greater than it
was before the late war.

That is not only a very serious thing for the cause of peace ultimately, but it constitutes an economic drain on the resources of Europe much too great for her in her present condition, and one which she can ill afford to bear.

The worst of it is that armaments breed armaments. If one country is armed, the next country is armed. If one increases its armament, the next country increases its armament. We read sometimes in the papers of terrible cases of human beings who have become addicted to some of those horrible drugs, morphine, cocaine or the like, and they go on taking more and more of them until they are ruined body and soul. We call them drug maniacs. I fear very much that there are still some armament maniacs left among the nations of the world. We who really seriously desire peace, who are not only talking about it, but wish to do something for it, let us consider for a moment what is the cause of this horrible state of things.

Well, the disease is a fearful one, but luckily, the diagnosis is simple. What keeps alive armaments is one thing and one thing only. It is the fear and suspicion of the nations for one another. That is at the bottom of most of the troubles that afflict our world at the present time. Yet the remedy is simple enough ; at any rate simple enough to pronounce. We must have a new spirit in international affairs. We must get rid of the idolatry of force.

We must get the nations to recognise—and many

millions of them do recognise it—that it is not force that counts in human affairs, but reason and persuasion. We all recognise that in our individual capacity. Force does not count in our individual lives. It is not a motive that really has any importance for us. If we look at the great organisation of a city like this, at the intricate arrangements that have to be made to enable life there to be carried on, they are not the result of force. It is not because you or those who live here are afraid of violence that they conform to the usages of civilised society. They do it voluntarily. The vast majority of their actions, the vast number of those proceedings which make life in a great city or life in the country possible, tolerable, for those who live there, are dictated by the most powerful influence in the world, the public opinion of your fellows. It governs your dress, it governs what you eat, it governs the games at which you play ; it governs almost everything you do, from your business to your pleasure, from morning until evening.

It is public opinion which governs—next to your self-respect and your own judgment of what is right —it is public opinion that governs you throughout the whole of your life. And what is true with individuals is true, or ought to be true, with nations, so that if you take the proper steps to concentrate, to develop and to publish public opinion throughout the world, a nation bent on a desperate effort to assassinate its neighbour will be restrained by the

obloquy of the whole civilised world. And the first
condition that is necessary for that is to get rid of
these vast and threatening armaments which prevent
the full power of public opinion throughout the
world.

Well, now, what are the conditions which it is
necessary to fulfil if you are to induce the nations of
the world to disarm? You have no great land
armaments in this country. Why? Because you
are not threatened by any neighbours who desire to
attack you—or not seriously threatened.

If you could get the same state of mind in Europe,
you would get the same result. If you could say to
the nations of Europe : " Don't be afraid. There
is no real danger. You may sleep quietly in your
beds. You may put off once for all this vast burden
of armaments. You may cease to create dangers
for your neighbours in the effort to create safety for
yourself." If we could say to the nations : " We
will give you security which will enable you to
dispense with armaments," then we could ask them
to disarm.

I believe that can be done. I believe it can be
done like this. Take a continent, a quarter of the
globe, like Europe ; if all the nations there were to
agree that if each of them reduced their armaments
to an agreed amount, all of them would come to the
assistance of any one of them who was attacked—
just think what a splendid advance that would be.
It would rule out aggressive attack for ever. Aggres-

sive attack would be so dangerous that no nation would ever undertake it. And if you get rid of aggression, you get rid of war, because war must begin by aggression on one side or the other. I am firmly convinced that an arrangement of that kind in Europe would be of enormous advantage, and I would like to see as part of that arrangement an agreement among the nations, at any rate among the nations who felt themselves in danger of attack, that there should be a zone between nation and nation, demilitarised and made incapable of being used without delay and preparation for the advance of an invading army, so that the guaranty offered to them by other nations in Europe would become effective before it was too late.

That is the kind of scheme by which I think security might be given. But it is evident that for that scheme to be effective, you must create or utilise some international authority. Disarmament to be effective must be general. You will never get one nation to disarm as long as other nations arm. If you are to carry out a general scheme of disarmament, you must have an international organisation to supervise it. If you are to have a scheme of zones, of demilitarised zones, you must have an international authority to overlook it. But you have got to do something much more than that, you have got to carry out and to apply—not to Europe only but to all nations—you have got to carry out a scheme of moral disarmament as well as material disarmament.

You have got to bring the nations together, to teach them that their common interests are far greater than their common antagonisms, to teach them that just as it is true of individuals that we are all parts one of another, and that if individuals in a great community suffer, then the whole community suffers ; so we must teach the nations of the world that they are all parts of one common whole, and that it is untrue, a devilish untruth, that there is any advantage to any one nation in the misfortunes or the poverty of others.

International co-operation is not only a proper object, it is inevitable. If there are more than a million men now out of work in England, it is, very largely if not entirely, because of the economic difficulties which exist in the rest of Europe. If the farmers of the United States are unable to sell their wheat at a remunerative price, it is because their customers in Europe are unable to buy it. The economic interdependence of the world is a great fact, it is not a thing about which we need argue, it is a fact which we cannot evade. And if the economic interdependence of the world is a fact, much more is the scientific, the intellectual, the moral interdependence of the world a fact also. Why, it may well be that some medical or scientific discovery in Europe will affect the lives of thousands of people in this country, just as some improvement in the works of civilisation here, transportation or what not, may brighten the lives of hundreds of thousands of people in Europe. Science and art and intellect and morals have no boundaries.

The world is one, humanity is one family ; that is a fact which no sophisms of political philosophers can ever alter or destroy. And therefore, as wise men, we must, as it seems to me, recognise that great fact. We must recognise that there are great common interests in the world, and we must do our best to provide for them. There are great moral evils which affect the whole world. There are great difficulties of inter-communication, there are great dangers of epidemic diseases, there are great diversities of social conditions which have their reaction on the prosperity and happiness of the people of every country. Let us recognise and work to diminish those common evils. Let us agree, if we can agree on nothing else, on joint international action to this end ; for the improvement of the lot of humanity in those ways is the interest not only of the whole world but of every nation that composes the world.

Therefore we must have, at any rate for those purposes, periodic meetings, conferences, discussions, some kind of machinery to make those discussions and conferences effective ; and, let us add, surely we may add, this : some kind of machinery for diminishing the danger of international disputes, and preventing disputes from degenerating into war. Is that so very unreasonable ? Does that really offend any of our prejudices, or any of our preconceived opinions? And that, as you all know, is fundamentally all that the League of Nations proposes to do.

The central idea of the League of Nations, as I understand it, is a system of international conferences and co-operation, not depending on coercion, without coercion, without force, without any interference with the sovereignty or full independence and freedom of action of any of its members, working not for any selfish interests, but for the establishment of better and more brotherly relations between the nations, and for the establishment of peace upon the earth. That is the idea of the League. I believe myself that in its broad lines the Covenant carries out that idea. But I am not bigoted about it, nor is any other intelligent advocate of the League. We don't say that the Covenant is perfect, or was inspired from heaven. We are prepared, all of us, to support amendments if amendments are required.

I myself believe that the theory that the League of Nations as established by the Covenant could be used in any way as a super-state is totally untrue. But if I am wrong and if it can be pointed out that there is any article in the Covenant which is justly open to such a charge, for what my assistance is worth, I tender it in support of any amendment that may be necessary to put it right. But I do beg those who criticise the League not to rest on *a priori* considerations. Let them not only read the Covenant, but let them, I beg them, study the working, the actual working of the League.

I assert that the League has already done much for the betterment of mankind. I assert that through its means hundreds of thousands of prisoners of war have been rescued from hardship and starvation. I assert that effective measures have been taken to prevent the spread of epidemics over Europe from the oppressed and miserable districts of Western Russia. I assert that more has been done in the three years since the League of Nations came into existence for putting an end to that terrible evil, the trade in noxious drugs, than has been done for fifty years before ; and I assert that with almost equal speed conventions have been agreed on through the instrumentality of the League which will really, I hope, put a spoke in the wheel of those devilish beings who carry on the white slave traffic. I assert that the League has been the means of settling several grave international disputes. I assert that in settling those disputes the League has shown a high impartiality, not hesitating to decide, if justice so required, in favour of the weaker rather than the stronger of the disputants.

I assert that the League's recommendations—and remember that the League only proceeds by recommendations, never by forcing its decisions on the people concerned—I assert that the League's recommendations have been accepted in almost every case. Let me give you one instance, well known, concerning a small country, but very striking—I refer to the case of Albania. What happened ? Here was a country, a little country of about a million inhabitants, just brought into existence, recognised by the League's efforts for the first time, struggling into statehood. It comes to the League. It asks for protection against a much larger neighbour. The League finds the larger neighbour has actually invaded Albania with its troops, that its troops are moving forward. The Council is summoned. The neighbour is warned that it must not continue to do what it is doing, it must not go to war until whatever grievances it has have been considered in a peaceful way. And instantly the neighbour withdraws all its troops, withdraws them without doing any harm to the country, withdraws them without anger, without that terrible feeling which so often results from international decisions reached by other means, and which leaves an open sore to break out afterwards and cause irreparable damage.

So little of the soreness existed in this case that the two nations immediately afterwards entered into a treaty of amity and commerce. And I myself heard the foreign minister of the invading state, speaking at the tribunal of the Assembly of the League, declare that the relations between the two countries were now excellent and friendly, and attribute that happy result to the mediation and influence of the League.

Now, it is all very well to say that Albania is a tiny country ; it is all very well to say that what can be done in a small country cannot necessarily be done carping spirit, but constructed with a desire to advance the great cause which I firmly believe the American people have as much at heart as any people in the world.

I do not venture to ask you to do anything ; but I will ask you one or two questions. I have no complaint or criticism at all, very much the reverse, for what America has done for Europe ; but has she done—I only ask it—has she done enough for herself ? She desires to avoid, no one can complain of it, entanglements in the affairs of Europe. She wishes to keep herself free from the wickedness and perversity, so I am told, of the rest of the world. But can she be free ? Is it possible for her to carry out that policy ? Why, in 1917 the people of America, I am sure, desired peace as much as any people in the world, as much as we English desired it ourselves. And yet, as I am informed by an almost unanimous national decision, she decided that it was essential for her to go into the war. It was essential, she thought, on that occasion. Suppose there is another world war, involving, as all world wars must involve, great questions of right and wrong. Are you sure that America will not feel herself forced, as she did in 1917, again to enter that war ? Is there anyone here who will tell me that the decision of 1917 was wrong ? I do not believe it. And if it was not wrong then, can they be certain that they will not be forced to an equally right decision in a future world war ? But if that were so, is it not intensely desirable that there should be no world war, even from the point of view of American interests ? Is it really true that she can afford to stand aside, and allow any kind of a disaster to happen in Europe, any kind of war to begin there, hoping, gambling on the chance that it will not so far extend as to compel her, be it by her moral or her material interests, to take her part ?

I ask you the question. It is for you to decide. And if you say, " Yes, there should be some safeguard against future war," then I do earnestly ask you, not to tell me but to tell yourselves, to think for your-selves what that safeguard should be ; whether there is some better safeguard than we, the fifty-two nations of the League, have devised for ourselves ; and if so, what are the alterations, what are the changes, what are the modifications that you think essential in order to make a satisfactory protection and safeguard against this overpowering evil ? For when war begins no one can limit its extent. That is the truth which history teaches, and which all intelligent men and women should recognise.

Well, I put to you those questions. In any case we in Europe must go on ; we cannot draw back from this great experiment. We are bound by every consideration of prudence and honour to pursue it to the end : prudence, because we see no other hopeful means to preserve our civilisation ; honour, because we who remain solemnly pledged ourselves to those who died that we would make it our first

I will not weary you with trying to enumerate the many gratifying aspects this event holds for me, but there is one to which I should wish to allude. The fact that it is connected with the name of Woodrow Wilson is a great element in the pride with which I regard it. I had the privilege of the acquaintance—may I not say friendship?—of Mr. Wilson, and I am not going to attempt any elaborate eulogy of him to-night. He was a very great man. He was a great American and a great citizen of the world. There is no title to fame higher than that. He possessed, as we all know, a very remarkable combination of the qualities of the student and the statesman, a rare combination and as admirable as it is rare. It gave to him not only the cultured eloquence which we all admire, but that capacity for action which is not always found with academic training. But beyond all this and beyond many other intellectual and moral qualities which he possessed, he was by the admission of all an idealist, that is to say, a man who set before him some definite object of achievement to attain which he thought no personal sacrifice too great. He knew his moments of great popularity, he knew his moments of adversity, and through all he maintained that steady course which the pursuit of ideals alone renders possible.

I have two pictures of him in my mind which will remain as long as I live. One is of his arrival in London after the armistice. I see crowded streets, cheering multitudes, all the marks of enthusiastic admiration which have rarely, if ever, been paid by the masses of my fellow-countrymen to one who was not one of their nation. No foreign statesman or foreign potentate has, I believe, ever been received as President Wilson was received at the end of 1918, and he was greeted not only for himself but because he embodied the passionate aspiration of the peoples of the world for peace. He was regarded as the apostle of peace, and as such he was received in London, in Rome and in Paris with unbounded enthusiasm.

Then I have another picture of him in a quiet house in Washington, where I saw him eighteen months ago. The contrast was striking. He was broken in health, he had no longer any official position, his power was apparently gone. He received me in private, labouring under grave physical disabilities, but his manner, his attitude of mind remained unchanged. There was the same courtesy, calm and dignified, which I had known when I called upon him in his Presidential lodgings in Paris, and he talked to me just as he had talked to me then. And as I rose to take leave I asked him something about my own doings in this country and whether he approved of them. He replied with his usual kindness. Then he added these remarkable words : " But remember we are winning. Make no concessions "—a very striking phrase. I am not here to express agreement or disagreement with its sense. Some will think it wise and others unwise, some will think it prudent and far-seeing and others will think it the reverse, but I cannot believe that there will be anyone who will not admire such an indomitable spirit, such lion-hearted courage. It is only to idealists that an attitude of that kind is possible; devotion to an idea, to something beyond and above one's self alone lends courage to that degree.

And what was this idea ? Peace ! Undoubtedly, but it was something more definite and precise than that. It was rather peace based on the unity, the solidarity of mankind, the idea that humanity was in the last analysis one, and that if they could be made conscious of this unity peace would be possible. I have another recollection of Mr. Wilson. This time it was in a not very large room in the Hotel Crillon at Paris, a meeting of the League of Nations Commission of the Peace Conference. Very hot and crowded it was, men from many nationalities being there, all representatives of the allies in the Great War, still affected by the war mind—ultra-nationalistic perhaps one may say of them—and in the course of some discussion President Wilson spoke to them, and to that audience, perhaps as difficult as it is possible to conceive, he urged this doctrine of the solidarity of mankind, finishing with a glowing phrase to the effect that in the future, it might be the distant future, the time would come when loyalty to humanity would be as imperative a duty as was now patriotism to one's country.   It was a moving appeal, and even that unresponsive assembly felt it so.   I do not, of course, pretend that the idea was a new one.   It is—is it not ?—at least 1924 years old ?   Since then, many of the noblest teachers, religious, moral, as well as political, have held it, but it was never put forward with greater force or greater conviction than by President Wilson. How has it fared ?

Let us look back to the state of things that existed before the war.   At that time undoubtedly the dominant conception of international relations was " every nation for itself and the devil take the hindmost."   No doubt there were exceptions. There had been efforts, such as the Red Cross movement at Geneva and the Hague Court of Arbitration, to humanise and even to facilitate arbitration instead of war.   There had been great international experiments too, of which the most celebrated of recent times was the effort to organise Europe for peace after the Napoleonic wars—often misleadingly referred to as the Holy Alliance.   That was a system of conferences between the great Powers of Europe which did much for peace, but broke down in 1822 for want of a definite constitution and continuous machinery such as that established by the Covenant of the League of Nations.   Later there were the arrangements known as the Concert of Europe for dealing with the affairs of South East Europe—a very vague and formless system which yet did something for peace while it lasted. On this side of the Atlantic, too, there was the Monroe Doctrine which has been of great if limited value for the same cause.

But these were essentially exceptions. The general international rule was the crudest form of the struggle for life. Unrestricted international rivalry was preached almost as a duty irrespective of the obvious fact that the only logical outcome of such a doctrine was war, sooner or later. International anarchy diversified by war was, broadly speaking, the pre-war system. No one can doubt the evil of that state of things. It was portentous, menacing to civilisation itself. Its danger had been demonstrated to all but the blindest by the World War, and it was obvious that if it was to be cured, or even mitigated, some new conception of international relations, some insistence on the real unity of mankind, must be pressed upon the world.

Nor was the success of such an enterprise so hopeless as some may think it at first, for after all the desire for unity, for corporate life, is one of the strongest of human instincts, as strong as the opposite instinct of competition. We see it at work in a thousand forms in our national life. It is the basis of a vast number of our institutions, of our schools, our colleges, our states, our nations, our churches, and it does not seem in itself impossible that this great force should be used to bring about an increased solidarity of mankind. Obviously, if that is to be done, the first thing is to foster international co-operation by all means in our power. Do not mistake me. That is not to weaken patriotism. There is no opposition between this conception of international co-operation and that of patriotism. Indeed, no man will be a good citizen of the world unless he has shown himself a loyal and devoted citizen of his country. The nations can only unite with one another if they are already firmly united in themselves. Nor am I claiming that the League of Nations is the only expression of the new conception of international solidarity. On the contrary there have been other manifestations of the same spirit in the recent past, though I am myself convinced that it is only through permanent machinery continuously operating, such as you have in the League, that you can hope for a really effective expression of world unity. That is why I am so profoundly convinced that Mr. Wilson was wise in insisting that the Covenant of the League should form the first part, the essential foundation—at once, the corrective and the basis—of the peace treaties signed at Paris. But the principles which underlie the Covenant extend beyond its actual terms, and in what I am about to say I shall pray in aid all recent examples of international co-operation, whether the fruit of the League machinery or not. For in attempting a survey of world movements the widest outlook is the best.

Let me say at once with great confidence and profound conviction that in the last five years the advance in the direction of international co-operation has been little short of marvellous. Much of the work has been done so smoothly that it has escaped notice, and I am not going to attempt to try even your patience by a complete catalogue of what has been accomplished. But even the broadest survey will bring to light the great extent of the work and how it has touched every branch of international relations. Some one told me the other day that in the first eight months of this year no fewer than seventy-six international conferences and commissions have met at Geneva dealing with every sort of topic. That is typical of what has been going on during the last five years.

Take, for instance, what may be called the social relations of nations. It is much, surely, to have rescued from imprisonment and banishment some 450,000 prisoners of war and restored them to their homes ; to have liberated many hundreds, if not thousands, of Christian women who had been interned in harems. Much, too, has been done in taking care of and repatriating tens of thousands of Russian refugees, and I might prolong the list of such undertakings considerably. Or take the questions of health. It is by co-operation of the nations of the world that the epidemics threatening Europe from the war-swept areas of Eastern Europe have been prevented. By the same agency are being carried out the valuable enquiries into such diseases as malaria and cancer, the standardisation of biological remedies such as sera and the interchange of medical officers amongst the nations of the world, so that they shall learn what has been done in other countries to cope with the problems which they also have to meet.   Or among the humanitarian activities of the League, take the struggle with that very difficult and complex question, the suppression of the traffic in noxious drugs such as opium and cocaine.   Even now, as we know, an international conference is sitting, and whatever its difficulties may be I am confident it will obtain important progress in that arduous struggle.   Nor does opium stand alone.   There is the still more terrible evil of the traffic in women and children, where much that has been of the greatest importance has already been achieved, and I hope the day is not far distant when that blot on our civilisation will be merely an evil memory.   So too with the troublesome and disgusting problem of obscene publications.   International agreement has been arrived at, and effective steps are being taken, to limit that pest as far as it is international in character.   In this connection the recent appointment of a Commission to enquire into the position of that hoary evil of slavery should not be forgotten.

So, too, in the economic sphere much has been done.   One of the first steps taken was the general economic conference at Brussels to examine the economic problems of the world left by the war, and on the basis of that examination most of the work

that has since been done has been built. There
have also been conferences to facilitate international
transit, to simplify and standardise the laws about
such matters as bills of exchange and commercial
arbitration. An attempt is even being made to
bring about an agreement to reform the absurdities
of the calendar. I merely give these as examples
which could be considerably extended and which
show how far international co-operation in matters
of this kind is going. More attention has been paid
to other activities, which are perhaps in themselves
not more valuable than those to which I have referred
—I mean the political questions that have been
submitted to the new methods and new spirit.
There was the peaceful and successful settlement of
the controversy between Sweden and Finland about
the possession and government of the Aland Islands.
There was the adjustment of the serious difficulties
between Albania and Servia, which stopped the
invasion of Albania and for a time at least restored
harmony to those two countries. There was the less
complete solution of the controversy between Poland
and Lithuania over the possession of Vilna, which at
any rate stopped actual hostilities. And there was
the much discussed settlement of the Silesian
question between Poland and Germany, which,
whatever may be said about some of its features, is
in practice working smoothly and well. More
recently we have seen an admirable piece of international work accomplished in the settlement of the

government of the territory of Memel, to which our Chairman to-night so splendidly contributed by his tact and wisdom. That was a controversy which had troubled Europe for two or three years and had defied the ordinary diplomatic methods of settlement. Yet, applying the new spirit and principle of international unity to it, bringing it into the atmosphere which prevails in Geneva when the representatives of nations come together, not to obtain victories over one another but to secure agreement —in that atmosphere the difficulties of the Memel question rapidly disappeared, and in three months the Commission presided over by Mr. Norman Davis was able to present for adoption a solution which bids fair to be permanent.

I must not forget in this connection to deal with one or two questions in which it has been alleged that the same success has not been attained. There is the Corfu incident of 1923. I think so far from that incident being a failure it is really one of the most distinguished successes of the new international conception. Here was a case of a bitter quarrel between two nations caused by an occurrence of the most deplorable character, the murder of four Italian officers on Greek territory. It was the kind of case which in the past had often produced, if not actual war, at any rate prolonged embitterment of international relations. After all, it was just such an incident as that which gave rise to the World War itself. Yet in a very few weeks the matter was granting part of the British demands. But it was succeeded by another Ministry, constitutionally appointed, which accepted the remainder. Internationally the incident was closed. Yet even so the British representative on the Council of the League felt that it would be in accordance with the new spirit of international relations publicly to offer to lay before the Council of the League a full statement and account of British action in Egypt if any member of the League desired that that should be done. To my mind that is one of the most striking testimonials to the progress of the idea of international unity that has yet taken place. Here was a matter admittedly outside the cognisance of the League, as to which the British Government was none the less ready to give explanations, because it desired to pay tribute to the international authority and position of the League Council. So far from the authority of the League being flouted, as some have ignorantly suggested, it has been openly and emphatically endorsed.

Closely allied with these strictly political questions have been a number of other activities of a politico-economic character—I refer of course to the great and so far brilliantly successful efforts for the reconstruction of Austria, and the not less successful proceedings in Hungary. There the principle of international co-operation has been used in order to bring assistance to struggling members of the family of nations ; in Austria by the international guarantee of a loan coupled with provisions for the rehabilitation of Austrian finance ; in Hungary by utilising the international machinery in order to restore to that country financial credit and confidence without any guarantee. Perhaps an even more striking instance is what has been and is being accomplished in Greece. There a state, not in serious financial difficulties, was suddenly faced with the terrific problem of providing for a great stream of national refugees equal to one-quarter of its whole population, suddenly thrust upon its shores by the fortune of war. The League—for it was done through the League—used its machinery to give confidence to the world that money lent to Greece would be applied in reproductive work for dealing with this great problem. As in Hungary we have had the assistance of distinguished American citizens to direct the operations in the country itself, and it has been to me extraordinarily striking that when the recent loan to Greece was put upon the London market it was recommended to the investors mainly upon the ground that since the League was taking an interest in its administration they might be satisfied that the money would not be wasted. I do not know how the loan went here, but in London it was subscribed fifteen times over within a couple of hours of its being offered.

There has, of course, been also the greatest of all the international reconstruction efforts, that for dealing with the Reparation question in Germany an arrangement between Greece and Bulgaria alien population of the two races in each country are to be exchanged, and the work is proceeding under the supervision of two Commissioners appointed by the League. Recently a minorities treaty came into force in the same districts, and the government agreed to entrust the same Commissioners with the supervision of the rights and obligations under these treaties also.

I must hurry on, but I cannot omit without any mention the great international institutions which have sprung up as part of the general scheme of international co-operation in close connection with the League. There is the International Labour Office, which aims at establishing standardised labour conditions of employment all over the world, so that no advantage shall accrue to any country by inhumane exploitation of labour. There is the Permanent Court of International Justice, where we have at last seen the fruition of ideas and efforts long and hitherto unsuccessfully made to create a genuine international court of justice. It is functioning with remarkable success and has already disposed of a number of international controversies which would otherwise have created a festering sore in the common life of the nations of the world. Then there is the Mandates Commission, where you have now a skilled international body to whom annual reports are presented on the administration of a number of territories inhabited by less advanced peoples, and where the principle has been accepted that the administering country is the trustee of its powers for the benefit of the inhabitants themselves and for the interest of the world at large. I wish I had time to describe more fully the work of the Mandates Commission, but anyone who has read their reports will agree with me that the sober, impartial, practical spirit that pervades them is of the happiest augury for the future of this very interesting experiment.

Quite recently two other very interesting international experiments have been begun. By the generosity of the French Government an institution fostering intellectual co-operation is to be established under the auspices of the League at Paris. Already valuable work has been done by some of the chief thinkers of the world in meeting together to discuss international intellectual problems, and this new institute is to strengthen and co-ordinate their exertions. Further, at the last Council meeting the Italian Government offered to establish an institution also under the League for considering the prospects of the unification of private law. This is not the codification of international law. But that object, the dream of so many an idealist, has not been forgotten. It is a difficult question, but a beginning has been made. At the last Assembly a small expert committee was appointed to study what subjects of international law are ripe for codification. The lines to be followed are somewhat those laid down by Mr. Elihu Root in the Commission which this question. It is, of course, the very heart of the matter. Disarmament is the goal to which all intelligent lovers of peace must desire to tend, but the difficulties in the way are prodigious and it will need all the new spirit of which I have spoken to secure success. To me the fact that the problem is taken seriously and is now being grappled with is in itself an immense encouragement, and I look confidently forward to substantial advances being actually secured in the course of the next few months.

Well, ladies and gentlemen, if I haven't wearied you, and you have been able consequently to follow what I have tried to say, I am sure you will agree with me that we who believe in peace and still more believe that it is a cause worthy of our utmost exertion, have much to be thankful for. Especially may those take courage who have felt the inspiration of the great ideal for which Woodrow Wilson was content to sacrifice his health and, alas, even his life. The advance which that ideal has made during the last five years has been greater than that of any similar human movement with which I am acquainted. We have to encourage us a record of great and even marvellous achievement, and we may look forward to an even greater promise for the future.

Nor must it be thought for an instant that in recounting the great work done by the League I have overlooked the splendid contribution made by America in recent years, as always, to the cause of world peace. I have already alluded to the Washington Conference on reduction of naval armaments, to the success of which Mr. Secretary Hughes and other distinguished American statesmen made such an invaluable contribution. Nor have I failed to note the splendid work done by our Chairman of to-night and by other individual Americans in the cause of world reconstruction, and other beneficent activities of international organs and agencies.

We in the Old World have never failed to recognise the strength of American devotion to peace and goodwill among the nations of the world. We know that you plan no conquests, that you nurse no ambition for territorial expansion. The unguarded Canadian frontier is a proof that we have no fear of American militarism. No nation in the world has stood so consistently for peace as yours. Nor will you hear from me one word of criticism as to your attitude towards the League, or any suggestion that it springs from lack of sincerity or conviction in your horror of war. No intelligent supporter of the League could do otherwise than recognise unreservedly that it is part of the essential sovereignty of each nation—a sovereignty which is the very basis of the League constitution—to settle for itself what shall be its external policy. That is for America and for America alone. We of the League have our task. We believe that to us has been entrusted a great mission for peace. We see that much has already been done and that still more remains to be accomplished. The seed planted by Woodrow

Wilson and his colleagues at Paris has already grown and flourished beyond the most sanguine expectation. Let it be ours to foster its growth, and not wasting our time in criticism or regret, let us press forward towards that glorious prize which even now seems almost within our grasp.

PRINTED IN GREAT BRITAIN BY ROBERT MACLEHOSE AND CO. LTD.
THE UNIVERSITY PRESS, GLASGOW.